Windows 2012 Server Network Security

Windows 2012 Server Network Security

Securing Your Windows Network Systems and Infrastructure

Derrick Rountree

Richard Hicks, Technical Editor

AMSTERDAM • BOSTON • HEIDELBERG • LONDON
NEW YORK • OXFORD • PARIS • SAN DIEGO
SAN FRANCISCO • SINGAPORE • SYDNEY • TOKYO

ELSEVIER

Syngress is an Imprint of Elsevier

SYNGRESS

Acquiring Editor: *Chris Katsaropoulos*
Editorial Project Manager: *Heather Scherer*
Project Manager: *Priya Kumaraguruparan*
Designer: *Mark Rogers*

Syngress is an imprint of Elsevier
225 Wyman Street, Waltham, MA 02451, USA

Notices
Knowledge and best practice in this field are constantly changing. As new research and experience broaden our understanding, changes in research methods or professional practices, may become necessary. Practitioners and researchers must always rely on their own experience and knowledge in evaluating and using any information or methods described herein. In using such information or methods they should be mindful of their own safety and the safety of others, including parties for whom they have a professional responsibility.

To the fullest extent of the law, neither the Publisher nor the authors, contributors, or editors, assume any liability for any injury and/or damage to persons or property as a matter of products liability, negligence or otherwise, or from any use or operation of any methods, products, instructions, or ideas contained in the material herein.

Library of Congress Cataloging-in-Publication Data
Application submitted.

British Library Cataloguing-in-Publication Data
A catalogue record for this book is available from the British Library.

ISBN: 978-1-59749-958-3

Printed in the United States of America
13 14 15   10 9 8 7 6 5 4 3 2 1

Contents

Dedication

This book is dedicated to my daughter Riley, the most amazing two-year-old ever.

Acknowledgments

I would like to thank my wife Michelle, my mother Claudine, and my sister Kanesha. I would also like to thank the Elsevier staff, especially Angelina Ward and Heather Scherer. It has truly been a pleasure working with you.

About the Author

Derrick Rountree (CISSP, CASP, MCSE) has been in the IT field for almost 20 years. He has a Bachelor of Science degree in Electrical Engineering. Derrick has held positions as a network administrator, an IT consultant, a QA engineer, and an Enterprise Architect. He has experience in network security, operating system security, application security, and secure software development. Derrick has contributed to several other Syngress and Elsevier publications on Citrix, Microsoft, and Cisco technologies.

About the Technical Editor

Richard Hicks is a network and information security expert specialized in Microsoft technologies, an MCP, MCSE, MCITP Enterprise Administrator, CISSP, and four-time Microsoft Most Valuable Professional (MVP). He has traveled around the world speaking to network engineers, security administrators, and IT professionals about Microsoft edge security and remote access solutions. A former information security engineer for a Fortune 100 financial services company in the US. He has nearly two decades of experience working in large-scale corporate computing environments. He has designed and deployed perimeter defense and secure remote access solutions for some of the largest companies in the world. Richard has served as a technical reviewer on several Windows networking and security books and is a contributing author for WindowsSecurity.com and ISAserver.org. He is an avid fan of Major League Baseball and in particular the Los Angeles Angels (of Anaheim!), and enjoys craft beer and single malt Scotch whisky. Born and raised in Southern California, he still resides there with Anne, the love of his life and wife of 27 years, along with their four children. You can keep up with Richard by visiting http://www.richardhicks.com/.

Preface

Windows 8 and Windows Server 2012 are major releases for Microsoft. There are a lot of new networking features and improvements to old features. We will be looking at these features from a security perspective. We will cover general functionality where necessary, but our focus will be on security. We will discuss how to secure your general networking features. We will also discuss how to implement security-related features.

You must keep in mind that security is not just about cryptography and virus protection. The basis of information security is the CIA triad. This includes confidentiality, integrity, and availability. We're going to discuss ways of making your networked systems secure, stable, and highly available.

This book is not an administrator's guide. We won't be going over where to find tools and utilities. We also won't be going over general configuration information, unless we are configuring a security-related feature. If you need in-depth information about features and functionality, it's recommended that you use supplemental reference material.

INTENDED AUDIENCE

This book is intended for anyone who will be using, administering, or securing Windows 8 or Windows Server 2012 systems and networks. In the past, security was just for security professionals. They were the only ones who cared about making sure systems were safe. Nowadays, we realize that everyone has a hand in making sure the environment is secure. A DNS Administrator, for example, must make sure that not only is the DNS infrastructure doing name resolution properly, but also that it's available when needed and is protected against unauthorized requests.

To get the full value from this book, an individual should have a good understanding of general networking concepts. You should also have a good understanding of how to administer Windows systems. Since the book will not be covering general Windows functionality, it's important to have an understanding of how to navigate the new look and feel of Windows system.

WHY IS THIS INFORMATION IMPORTANT

Nowadays, we realize it's everyone's responsibility to make sure the system they use is secure. With the release of a new operating system comes a new set of attacks. It's important that you have the right information needed to mitigate these attacks. This is what this book will provide you with.

The cyber world is evolving. Companies not only have to worry about external threats, but also internal threats. Attacks are becoming more complex and more calculated. Attackers don't always attack the system they want directly. They may compromise another system and use that system to attack their ultimate target. Even if you don't want a certain system to have valuable information on it, it still needs to be protected. You don't want that system to be the one used to compromise another system.

New initiatives like BYOD (Bring Your Own Device) are allowing corporate users to bring their personal devices into the workplace. This has caused a blur in the line between corporate and personal systems. You have both types of devices on the network. So, it's important that both types of devices be secured.

THE STRUCTURE OF THE BOOK

This book is broken down into seven chapters, including the Introduction. The chapters flow from infrastructure outward to Internet connectivity. Then it's wrapped up with the tools you need to monitor and administer these environments.

Chapter 1: Introduction

The Introduction will give you a general overview of the tools needed to manage Windows systems. We provide this overview to ensure that there is a good foundation for the concepts we cover later. We will also go over IPv6. The configuration and management of an IPv6 environment is different from an IPv4 environment. So we want to make sure you have a good understanding of some of the new concepts before we move forward.

Chapter 2: Network Infrastructure

This chapter will discuss how to securely deploy your network infrastructure. The infrastructure is what will provide the basis for the rest of your network connectivity. We will cover how to secure your DHCP, DNS, and WINS infrastructure.

Chapter 3: Securing Network Access

This chapter will cover how to connect a system to network. We will cover both wired and wireless access. We will go over to basic connectivity and access as well as to more advanced concepts like Windows Firewall and IPSec.

Chapter 4: Secure Remote Access

This chapter will cover remote access to your network and to individual systems. It's important that this be done in a secure way to prevent unauthorized access and information leakage.

Chapter 5: Internet Connection Security

In this chapter, we will discuss how to secure Internet Connections. We will start with Internet Explorer and then move to general Internet security settings.

Chapter 6: Network Diagnostics and Troubleshooting

In this chapter, we will cover tools that can be used to monitor and troubleshoot your systems. They can be used to help ensure availability. They can also be used to detect unwanted or malicious activity.

Chapter 7: Network Tools and Utilities

This chapter discusses some of the network tools and utilities that can be used to configure, manage, and secure Windows networking components. We will cover some simple command-line utilities as well as more robust tools.

CHAPTER 1

Introduction

- Intro to Windows 8 and Windows Server 2012
- Intro to IPv6

CONTENTS

Networking is a key component of any environment. Windows 8 and Windows Server 2012 offer a wide range of networking features and functionality. It's important that you understand these features and functionality so that you can properly secure them. But, before we get into those, we will start with some more general information. In this chapter, we will start with an overview of some of the key components of Windows 8 and Windows Server 2012 that will help you as we go through the rest of the chapters. Then we will move into a discussion of IPv6, and how it's implemented in Windows 8 and Windows Server 2012.

INTRO TO WINDOWS 8 AND WINDOWS SERVER 2012

When you look at Windows 8 and Windows Server 2012, the first thing you will notice is a big difference in the UI. But, that's not the only difference. There are some important differences in the management of the operating systems. There is a new Server Manager console that offers new management functionality and there has been increased functionality built into Powershell.

Server Manager

In Windows Server 2012, Server Manager has been enhanced to provide greater management and monitoring functionality. It's your starting point for a lot of general administrative functions you will need to perform. You can access event and performance information. You can also install new roles and services from here.

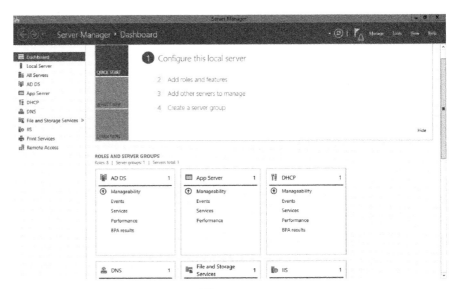

FIGURE 1.1 Server Manager Dashboard View

Dashboard

When you log into Windows Server 2012, Server Manager will open. You will be presented with the Dashboard view, as seen in Figure 1.1. The Dashboard view allows you to access information about different roles and services that have been installed on the system. You can view information on manageability, events, performance, and BPA results.

Local Server

The Local Server section, as seen in Figure 1.2, will give you detailed information about the server to which you are currently connected. You can view server properties, events, services, Best Practices Analyzer information, performance information, and roles and features information.

Add Roles and Features

Server Manager is where you go to Add Roles and Features to your server. In upcoming chapters, we will be installing different roles and features. Most of these installs will be launched from Server Manager. The first few steps of all the installs will be the same. So, instead of repeating these steps multiple times, we will go through these steps now:

1. In the Server Manager Dashboard, select Add Roles and Features. This will launch the Add Roles and Features Wizard. First, you will be presented with the Before You Begin screen, as seen in Figure 1.3. This screen describes what can be done using the wizard. It also gives configuration suggestions to follow before you continue with the wizard. Click Next.

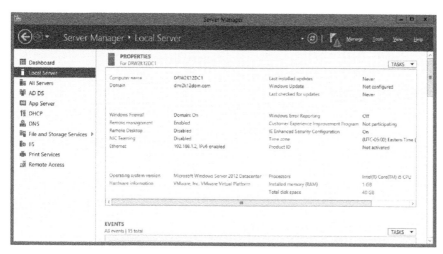

FIGURE 1.2 Server Manager Local Server View

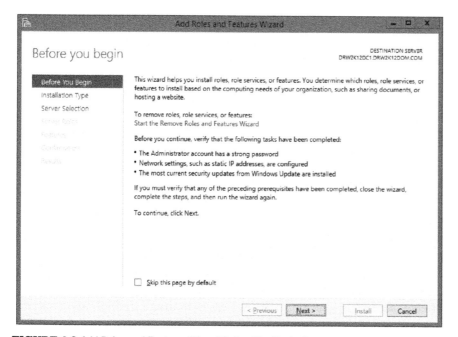

FIGURE 1.3 Add Roles and Features Wizard Before You Begin Screen

2. Next, you will see the Installation Type screen, as seen in Figure 1.4. You have two options. You can install roles or features on the system; or you can install VDI (Virtual Disk Infrastructure) services on the system. Select **Role-based or feature-based installation**, and click Next.

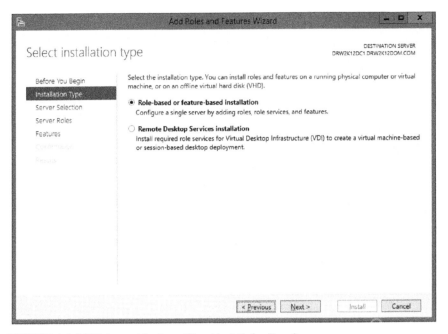

FIGURE 1.4 Add Roles and Features Wizard Installation Type Screen

3. Next you will see the Server Selection screen, as seen in Figure 1.5. Here, you can choose to install to a server or to a VHD (virtual hard disk). If you choose a VHD, you have the option to install to a VHD attached to an online server, or to install to an offline VHD. Select **Select a server from the server pool**. Then choose the server you want to install onto, and click Next.

Config Export

One useful feature of the Roles and Features Wizard is the ability to export an installation configuration. After you have finished configuring the settings for an installation, you have the option to save the configuration to an XML file. You can then use Powershell to script an install with the same settings on a different server. This not only makes it easier to install multiple servers, but it also helps to ensure consistent installations. The command you would use to perform the install is as follows:

Install-WindowsFeature-ConfigurationPathFile <exportedconfig.xml>.

Notifications

The Notifications section of Server Manager, as seen in Figure 1.6, will provide notification and alert messages. For example, after you install a role,

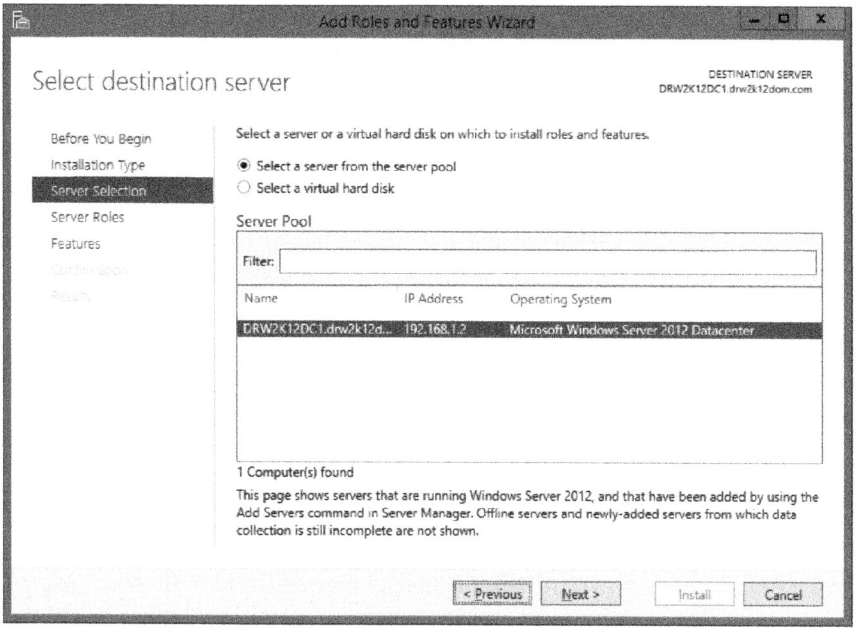

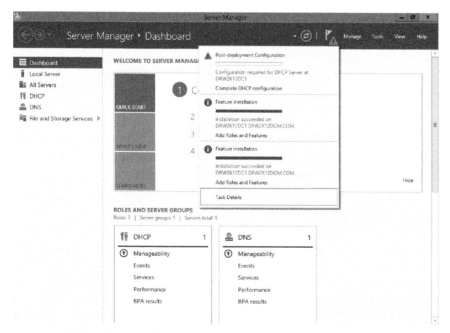

FIGURE 1.5 Add Roles and Features Server Selection Screen

FIGURE 1.6 Server Manager Notifications Sections

a notification will be posted letting you know that the install was successful. You will also get a notification after an install, if there is post-install configuration that needs to be done.

Manage

The Manage menu provides you the ability to add and remove roles and features. You can add servers to be managed by Server Manager. You can also create server groups.

Tools

The Tools menu brings up a list of various tools that you can use to manage your server. There are entries for Local Security Policy, Performance Monitor, Resource Monitor, the Security Configuration Wizard, and many other options. Some of these security-related tools will be covered later in this book.

Powershell

Powershell is a very powerful management language used with Windows system. Windows Powershell is a combination command-line shell and scripting language. Powershell allows access to COM and WMI management components. This greatly expands the potential of the Powershell language.

Powershell is one of the main tools used for managing Windows systems. In fact, many Windows management consoles are actually built on top of Powershell. Powershell includes a hosting API that can be used by GUI applications to access Powershell functionality. Powershell commands can be executed as cmdlets, Powershell scripts, Powershell functions, and standalone executables. The Powershell process will launch cmdlets within the Powershell process. Standalone executables will be launched as a different process. As Windows moves forward, there will be an increasing reliance on Powershell. It's important that you understand how to use it to manage and administer your systems. As we go through this book we will periodically reference different Powershell commands than may be useful to you.

INTRO TO IPv6

IPv6 is the newest version of the IP protocol. It was designed to replace IPv4, which is the version used throughout most of the Internet. The problem was that there weren't enough IPv4 addresses to satisfy the needs of the growing Internet. IPv6 has been long talked about, but it is just now picking up steam. More and more Internet Service Providers are supporting the protocol. World IPv6 Launch Day was June 6, 2012. This was the day many ISPs and vendors permanently enabled IPv6 on for their products and services.

IPv6 Architecture

The IPv6 architecture is very different from the IPv4 architecture. These architecture differences are what make IPv6 the choice for the future. IPv6 is scalable, secure, and relatively easy to set up.

IPv6 Addressing

IPv6 addresses are 128 bits long. Compare that to IPv4 addresses which are 32 bits. This means there are 3.4×10^{38} addresses. That's approximately 4.8×10^{28} addresses for each person on earth. There is almost no way we will ever use anywhere near that many addresses. The main benefit of having that many addresses available is that you can waste addresses. With IPv4 addresses, there was no room for waste. You had to make sure you made the most efficient use of addresses possible. With IPv6, that's no longer a concern. You should make sure you come up with a scheme that is best for your organization, but it's ok if you waste addresses.

IPv6 Notation

IPv6 addresses consist of eight groups of 16-bit numbers, separated by colons. The 16-bit numbers are represented as hex digits:

    abcd:1234:1234:abcd:0230:0bcd:1234:a0cd

As you can see IPv6 addresses can be quite long and very hard to remember. To make things a little bit easier, IPv6 addresses can be abbreviated. There are two ways IPv6 addresses which can be abbreviated. The abbreviations are based on the existence of zeros. First of all you can remove one or more leading zeros from a group of 4 hex digits:

    abcd:1234:0000:abcd:0230:0bcd:1234:a0cd

becomes

    abcd:1234:0:abcd:230:bcd:1234:a0cd

Also, you can remove an entire section of zeros and replace with a double colon (::). The double colon can only be used once in an address:

    0000:0000:abcd:1234: abcd:1234:abcd:1234

becomes

    ::abcd:1234: abcd:1234:abcd:1234

or

    abcd:1234:0000:0000:0000:abcd:1234:abcd

becomes

    abcd:1234::abcd:1234:abcd

In IPv4 you had the network portion of the address and the host portion of the address. The subnet mask is used to tell you which portion of the address is which. There are two ways to write IPv4 subnet masks. You can use the traditional form, 255.255.255.0, for example. Or you can use the CIDR format, /24. In IPv6, the network portion of the address is called the prefix. The prefix is also denoted by the subnet mask. But, IPv6 subnet masks are only written using the CIDR format.

IPv6 Address Types

There are three types of addresses used with IPv6: unicast, multicast, and anycast. Unicast addresses are what you would call regular addresses. They are the addresses usually bound to your network card. Unicast addresses should be unique on a network, meaning a single unicast address should only represent a single system. Multicast addresses are used to make a one-to-many connection. Multiple systems can listen on the same multicast address. So, when a system sends out a message using a multicast address, multiple systems may respond. Multicast addresses will start with FF0 or FF1. FF02::2 is the multicast address used by routers. IPv6 uses multicast addresses to accomplish a lot of the functionality performed by broadcast addresses in IPv4. Anycast addresses are addresses that are shared by multiple system. Anycast addresses are generally used to find network devices like routers. When a message is sent out via an anycast address, any system using that address may respond.

Unicast addresses come in four flavors: global, site-local, link-local, and unique local. Global addresses are routable throughout the Internet. Global IPv6 addresses start with 001. Site-local addresses are only routable within a specified site within an organization. Link-local and unique local addresses will be covered in the next section on special addresses.

Note: The concept of sites has been deprecated in IPv6, so site-local addresses are no longer used.

IPv6 Special Addresses

There are several special addresses in IPv6. These addresses or groups of addresses serve very specific function. We will cover the loopback address, link-local addresses, and unique local addresses.

Loopback Address

The loopback address, also called localhost, is probably familiar to you. It is an internal address that routes back to the local system. The loopback address in IPv4 is 127.0.01. In IPv6, the loopback address is 0:0:0:0:0:0:0:1 or ::1.

Link-Local Addresses

Link-local addresses are intended to only be used on a single network segment or subnet. Routers will not route link-local addresses. Link-local addresses also existed in IPv4. They existed in the address block 169.254.0.0/16. These addresses were used by the DHCP autoconfiguration service on a system when a DHCP address could not be obtained. Link-local addresses allow you to have network connectivity until another more suitable address can be obtained. In IPv6, the address block fe80::/64 has been reserved for link-local addresses. The bottom 64 bits used for the address are random. In IPv6 link-local addresses may be assigned by the stateless address autoconfiguration process. IPv6 system must have a link-local address in order for some of internal protocol functions to work properly. So, during a normal startup process, an IPv6 system will obtain a link-local address before it receives a regular, routable IP address.

Unique Local Address

Unique local addresses are a set of addresses that are intended for use in internal networks. They are similar to "private" IPv4 addresses. These addresses can only be used within a specified organization. They are not routable on the global Internet. Using unique local addresses can help prevent external systems from having direct access to your internal systems. The address block fc00::/7 has been reserved to use for unique local addresses.

IPv6 Addressing

When you look at the IP configuration on an IPv6 system, you will see multiple addresses. First you will see the public address. The public address is the address used by other systems to contact an IPv6 system. This is the address that would be registered in the DNS server. You will also see what is called a temporary address. It's called temporary because it may change after a given interval. The temporary address is the address used when making connections to other systems, such as when you browse the Internet. This adds an additional layer of security because it would be very difficult to trace this temporary address back to the originating system.

Note: On Windows systems, the public address is simply label IPv6 address.

The third type of address you may see is a tentative address. After the system generates an address, it is considered tentative until the verification process to make sure the address does not exist elsewhere on the network completes. The verification process happens so quickly that you will probably never actually see an address labeled tentative.

Stateless Address Autoconfiguration

IPv6 systems can automatically configure themselves when on a network with an IPv6 compliant router. The process is as follows:

1. The system boots up and generates a link-local address.
2. A message is sent to the multicast address FF02::2 to find a router.
3. The router sends back a link address or prefix.
4. The system uses the prefix as the beginning portion of the address and randomly generates the ending portion of the address.

SUMMARY

Windows 8 and Windows Server 2012 have many similarities to older versions of Windows, but there are also many new aspects. There are new features and improvements on old features. The new Server Manager offers an improved management interface. There are also improvements to Windows Powershell that greatly expand its effectiveness.

IPv6 has been around for a while. It's also been supported in Windows systems for quite some time. But, as IPv6 grows in popularity, it's essential that you have a good understanding of it and how it works on Windows systems.

CHAPTER 2

Network Infrastructure

INFORMATION IN THIS CHAPTER

- DHCP
- DNS
- WINS

CONTENTS

INTRODUCTION

Protecting your network infrastructure is crucial to having a secure network. If the infrastructure is compromised, then all the systems that use the infrastructure are at risk. Windows servers can provide many of the components critical to your network infrastructure. Three of the most important components are DHCP, DNS, and WINS. We will discuss each of these in this chapter.

DHCP

DHCP is the Dynamic Host Configuration Protocol. It's similar to BOOTP, the bootstrap protocol. Simply put, DHCP is used to dynamically deliver network configuration information to clients. Many people think of DHCP as simply delivering IP configuration information. But, it's much more than that. You can use DHCP to push proxy configuration information, hard disk configuration information, and much more.

DHCP Overview

The DHCP process itself is somewhat unsecure. It starts with a broadcast, and that is where the danger starts. It's hard to protect a process that uses broadcast messages.

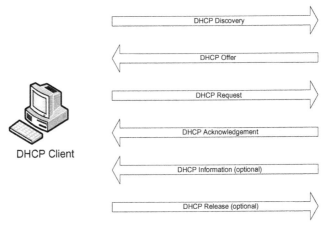

DHCP Client   DHCP Server

FIGURE 2.1 The DHCP Process

As seen in Figure 2.1, DHCP works as follows:

1. *DHCP Discovery:* The DHCP client will send out a broadcast message looking for DHCP servers on the network subnet.
2. *DHCP Offer:* A DHCP server will reserve an IP address and respond to the client with an offer for that IP address.
3. *DHCP Request:* The DHCP client will then send a message directly to the DHCP server that offered them an IP address with a request for usages of that address.
4. *DHCP Acknowledgment:* The DHCP sends back an acknowledgment of the request, the DHCP lease duration, and any other configuration information requested.
5. *DHCP Information* (optional): After the initial configuration, the DHCP client may request additional information from the DHCP server, such as WPAD information to find the location of a proxy server.
6. *DHCP Releasing* (optional): After the client has finished using the IP address it was assigned, it will send a release message to the DHCP server. This lets the DHCP server know that the IP can now be re-used and assigned to someone else.

DHCP Installation and Initial Configuration

Before you install your DHCP server, there is one very important thing you should consider. You should think about where you are going to install the DHCP server. DHCP servers are very vulnerable to various types of attackers. Because of this, you may want to think twice before you install DHCP on a server that has another critical service like your domain controller. If you're

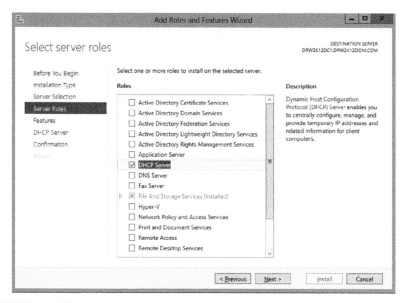

FIGURE 2.2 DHCP Server Role

installing in a POC or lab environment, it's probably okay. But, in a production environment, it's not recommended.

Adding the DHCP Server Role

To add the DHCP Server role, do the following:

1. On the Server Roles screen, as seen in Figure 2.2. This is where you will choose the DHCP Server role. After selecting the DHCP Server role, the wizard will pop up a window warning you of mandatory features that need to be installed with DHCP, as seen in Figure 2.3. Click Add Features. This will take you back to the Server Roles screen. Ensure DHCP server is selected and click Next.
2. Next, you will see the Features Screen. Click Next.
3. Next, you will see the DHCP server information screen as seen in Figure 2.4. This screen gives you a brief overview of the functions of a DHCP server. It also makes a couple of suggestions of steps that should be completed before you install and configure your DHCP server. Click Next.
4. Finally, you will see the Confirmation screen, as seen in Figure 2.5. On this screen, the wizard tells you which roles and features are going to be installed. Click Install to begin the installation.
5. The Roles and Features Wizard will track the progress of your installation. This can be seen on the Results screen as seen in Figure 2.6.

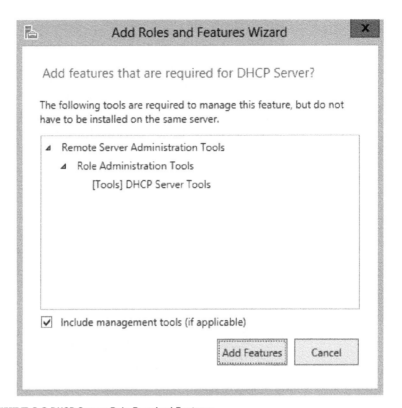

FIGURE 2.3 DHCP Server Role Required Features

FIGURE 2.4 DHCP Server Role Information

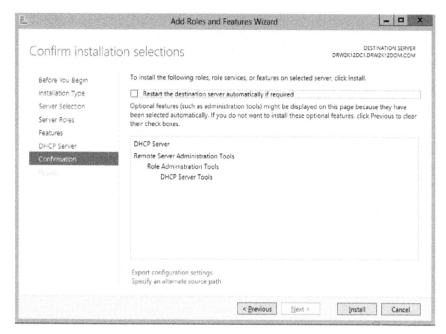

FIGURE 2.5 DHCP Confirmation Screen

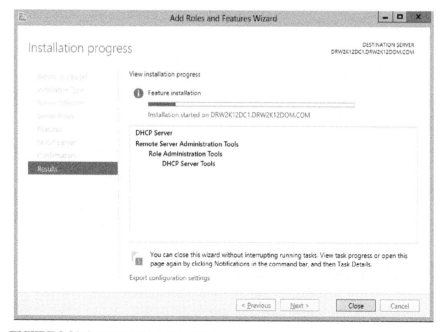

FIGURE 2.6 In Progress DHCP Role Installation

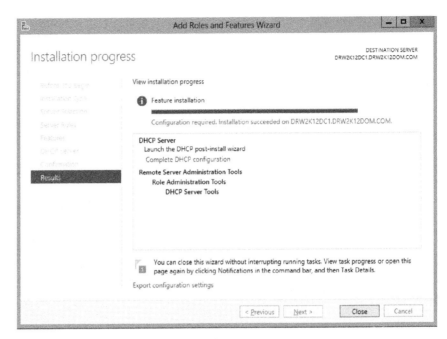

FIGURE 2.7 Completed DHCP Role Installation

6. At the end of the installation, the Results screen will tell if the installation was successful, as seen in Figure 2.7.

Initial DHCP Configuration

After you have installed the DHCP Server role, there is still configuration that needs to done. If you check the alerts in Server Manager, as seen in Figure 2.8, you will see that the post-deployment configuration must be done.

DHCP Post-Installation Configuration:

1. Selecting Complete DHCP Installation from Server Manager Alerts will bring up the DHCP Post-Install configuration wizard, as seen in Figure 2.9.
2. The Description screen lets you know what tasks the wizard is going to perform. It will create two security groups: DHCP Administrators and DHCP Users. The wizard will also authorize the DHCP server in Active Directory. Click Next.
3. Next you will be presented with the Authorization screen, as seen in Figure 2.10. This is where you will specify the credentials that will be used to authorize your DHCP server in Active Directory Services.

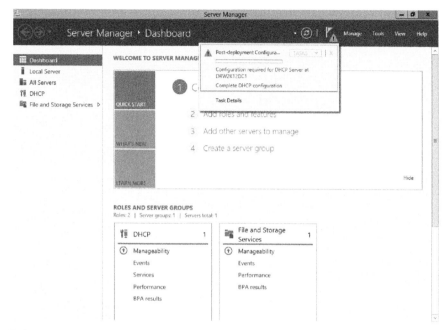

FIGURE 2.8 DHCP Post-Installation Alert

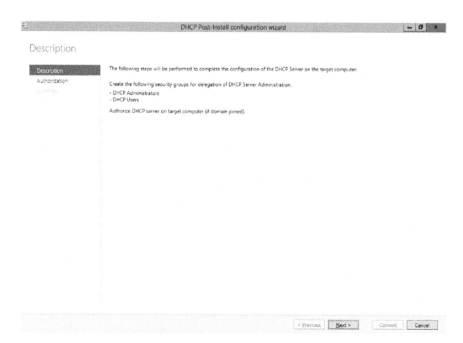

FIGURE 2.9 DHCP Post-Install Configuration Wizard

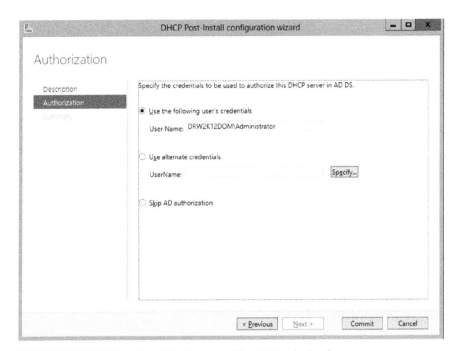

FIGURE 2.10 DHCP Post-Install Configuration Wizard Authorization Screen

You can use the current user's credentials, specify other credentials, or skip Active Directory authorization. Click Commit.

4. The summary screen as seen in Figure 2.11 will show you the status of the post-install wizard tasks. After all the tasks have been completed, click Close.

After you have installed and done the initial configuration for your DHCP server, you will notice that two logical DHCP servers show up in the DHCP Management Console. There is a logical server representing DHCP for IPv4 clients and a logical server representing DHCP for IPv6 clients.

Protecting Your DHCP Environment

Protecting DHCP can be somewhat difficult. The main problem is that DHCP is by design anonymous. DHCP requests aren't authenticated. You do not know who is making the request or who is servicing the requests. There are some methods that can be used to secure the requests and the responses and we will cover some of these in this section.

With DHCP, you need to protect your environment from the client side and server side. If your DHCP server is compromised, an attacker may use it to attack your clients. They may push out bogus IP addresses. This could prevent your clients from being able to connect your network, effectively delivering a

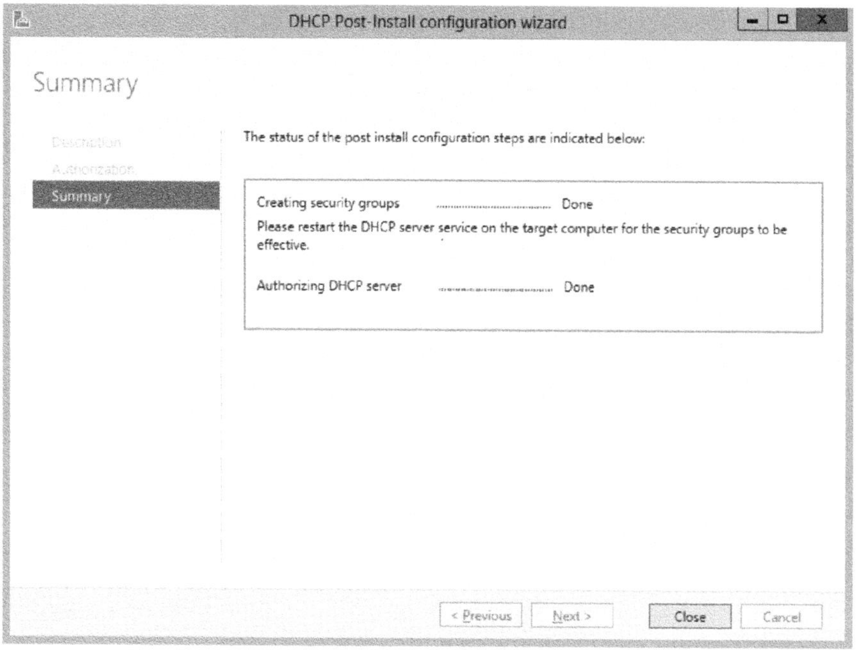

FIGURE 2.11 DHCP Post-Install Configuration Wizard Summary Screen

Denial of Service attack. An attacker could also use the server to push out DNS information that points to a malicious DNS server. This DNS server could be used to point clients to malicious attack sites.

It's also possible to attack your DHCP server from the client side. An attacker could use a client system to flood your DHCP server with requests. Then it may have a problem servicing valid requests. A malicious client system could also use a MAC address generation software to register a bunch of bogus MAC addresses with IP addresses. You could then end up in a situation where there are no IP addresses left for valid clients to use.

Reserved IP Addresses

Sometimes systems will require a dedicated IP address. This could be necessary in the case of firewall entries or certain application configurations. One option is to avoid DHCP altogether. This can be done through the use of static IP addressing. You can manually configure the IP information of your systems. This would include the required information like IP address and subnet mask. And also option information like default gateway and DNS server address. The problem with this is that every server has to be configured individually; not only for the initial configuration, but also if there are any configuration changes that need to be made.

One option some people take is to use DHCP reservations. With DHCP reservations, IP addresses are assigned to specific systems, usually via MAC address. When a system that has a reserved address requests an IP address through DHCP, the DHCP server will assign it the reserved address. With DHCP reservations, you can still use DHCP to push out the IP addresses and other IP configuration information. This makes it much easier when you have to make configuration changes. DHCP reservations give you the best of both worlds. There is some overhead in configuring DHCP reservations. You have to manually configure the reservations, so you will need to know the MAC addresses of the client systems. Because you need to know the MAC of the DHCP clients, you cannot use DHCP reservations with completely anonymous clients. For example, if you have a network where guest systems will be connecting, DHCP reservations will not work.

DHCP reservations are made by right-clicking on the Reservations folder under the DHCP scope and selecting New Reservation. To make a DHCP reservation for an IPv4 address, you must enter the following information, as seen in Figure 2.12:

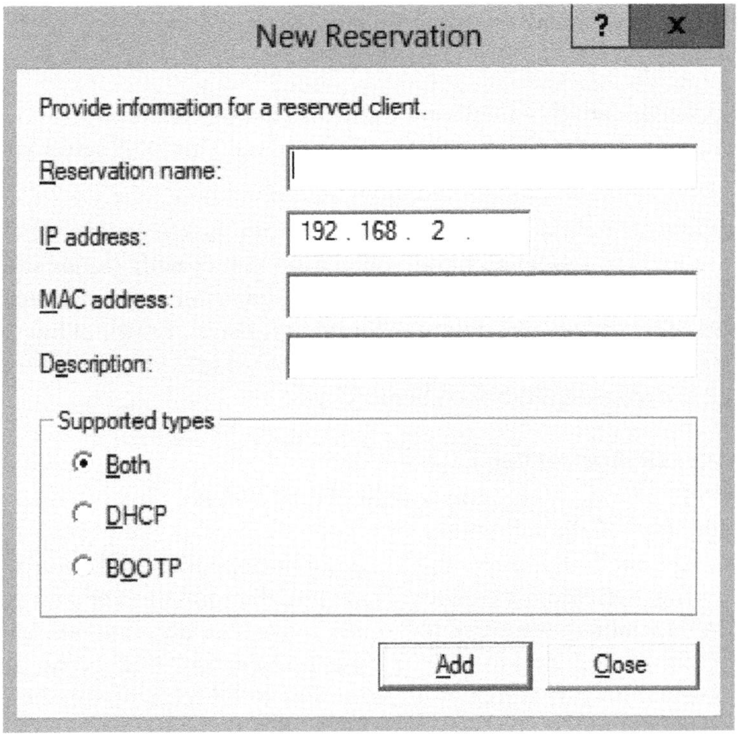

FIGURE 2.12 IPv4 DHCP Reservation

- *Reservation name:* Here you can specify a friendly name to denote the reservation. But, depending on your configuration, this name may automatically be overwritten with the system hostname.
- *IP address:* This is the IP address you want to assign.
- *MAC address:* This is the MAC address of the client system's network card.
- *Description:* This is a short description describing the reservation and possibly why it was done.
- *Supported types:* This is the type of request to respond. Request for IP configuration information can be made using the DHCP or BOOTP protocol.

To make a DHCP reservation for an IPv6 address, you must enter the following information, as seen in Figure 2.13:

- *Reservation:* This is the name used for the reservation.
- *IPv6 Address:* This is the IP address you want to assign.
- *DUID:* This is the DHCP Unique Identifier. It's automatically created by the client and is used as identification by the DHCP server.
- *IAID:* This is the Interface Association Identifier. It is a binding between an interface and an IP address.

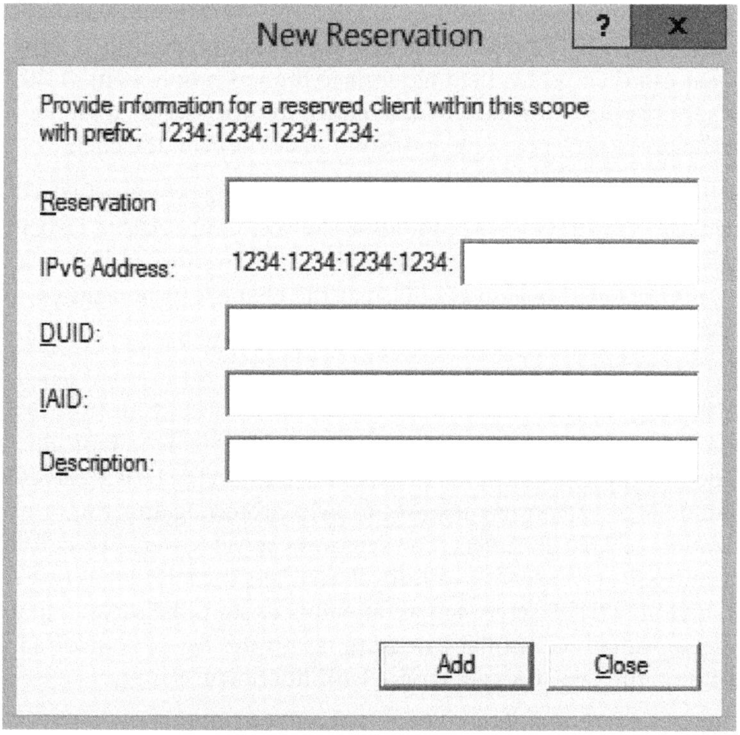

FIGURE 2.13 IPv6 DHCP Reservation

- *Description:* This is a short description describing the reservation and possibly why it was done.

Physical Security

Some people find that physical security and network entry point security work best for DHCP server. For physical security, you need to secure physical access to your DHCP server. Make sure your DHCP server is locked in a secure server room. Also, make sure the console itself is password protected. Protecting the network entry point means limiting who can access the network. You can lock down your network switches so that only specified clients can access the network.

Rogue DHCP Servers

One of the biggest problems facing DHCP is the presence of rogue DHCP servers. Rogue DHCP servers are DHCP servers that have been added to your network with permission. The rogue DHCP will respond to client requests. These rogue DHCP servers can cause Denial of Service attacks. They may respond to client invalid IP configuration information. So any clients receiving their configuration from one of these rogue DHCP servers will not be able to make connections via the network. A rogue DHCP could also respond with valid, but harmful information. For example, the DHCP server may respond to a client request with a DNS server address that points to a malicious DNS server. An attacker can then point client requests to the server they want. If the DHCP server responds with information for a malicious proxy server, then the attacker can use the proxy server to view network traffic sent from the client.

One method of combatting rogue DHCP servers is the process of DHCP server authorization. Windows environments allow you "authorize" a DHCP server. Only certain domain-based administrators are allowed to authorize a DHCP server. Once a DHCP is authorized, then the clients can be assured that the DHCP server it is talking to is a valid one.

Authorizing DHCP Servers

A rogue DHCP server attack is relatively simply to implement. Basically, all you have to do is connect a system to the network and start the DHCP server service. Windows does provide a few features to help protect against this. One is the authorization of DHCP servers. On Windows server systems since Windows 2000, the DHCP server service will not start unless the DHCP has been authorized. When the DHCP server service attempts to start, the server will attempt to contact a domain controller to ensure it's on the list of authorized DHCP servers. If not, the DHCP server service will shut down.

DHCP servers can be authorized during the post-install configuration wizard, using the DHCP Management Console, or via powershell. To authorize a

DHCP server in the DHCP Management Console, right-click on the server and select Authorize.

Conversely, if you are decommissioning a DHCP server, it should be unauthorized. To unauthorize a DHCP server in the DHCP Management Console, right-click on the server and select Unauthorize.

DHCP Snooping

DHCP snooping is used to protect your network against ARP spoofing and rogue DHCP servers. With DHCP snooping, the DHCP server and the layer 2 network switch work together to provide a secure layer 2 network environment. In DHCP snooping, there is a whitelist of IP addresses that can access the network. The layer 2 switch will track the MAC address and the port used by a particular system using an IP address. If the switch receives a request that does not match it's mapping, then the request is rejected.

Note: Enabling DHCP option 82 will cause information to be echoed that will help the switch in building its whitelist.

DHCP Audit Logging

DHCP auditing can provide you tons of useful information about what's going on with your DHCP implementation. The difficult part might be figuring out how to interpret the information.

To configure DHCP audit logging, perform the following steps:

1. In the DHCP Management Console, right-click on the DHCP server and select Properties.
2. On the General tab, check the box for Enable DHCP audit logging.
3. Click OK.

By default the DHCP audit logs are located in the %systemroot%\dhcp folder. There will be a different log for each day. There will also be a different log for each IP version you are running (v4 or v6). For example, the file DhcpSrvLog-Fri will have IPv4 entries created on Friday. The file DhcpV6SrvLog-Tue will have IPv6 entries created on Tuesday. The location of the logs can however be changed on the Advanced tab of server properties.

The log will contain a list of event IDs that you can use to figure out what the entries mean. Some of the codes that you might want to look out for from a security standpoint are:

13 The IP address was found to be in use on the network.
14 The lease request could not be satisfied because the scope's address pool was exhausted.
15 A lease was denied.

22 A dynamic BOOTP request could not be satisfied because the scope's address pool for BOOTP was exhausted.
23 A BOOTP IP address was deleted after checking to see it was not in use.
33 Packet dropped due to NAP policy.

Note: You need to make sure you take a look at the logs in a "clean" environment first. This will help give you an idea of what you can expect to see. Entries out of the norm could indicate an issue. For example, multiple bad addresses can indicate conflicts and rogue DHCP servers.

DHCP Administrators

To help with DHCP server administration, Windows includes the DHCP Administrators group. Users in this group will have rights to manage your DHCP servers. You can use this group for delegated administration. You don't have to give a user full administrator access to allow them to manage your DHCP server. To provide even more constrained access, Windows includes the DHCP Users group. Users in this group are given read-only access to the DHCP server management console.

DNS Settings

DHCP servers can be configured to register your clients in DNS. After the DHCP server assigns an address to the client, it will then register the system name and IP address mapping with the DNS server. The DNS registration settings are slightly different for IPv4 and IPv6 clients.

The DNS registration settings for IPv4 clients are as follows:

- Enable DNS dynamic updates according to the settings below:
    - Dynamically update DNS A and PTR records only if requested by the DHCP clients.
    - Always dynamically update DNS A and PTR records.
- Discard DNS A and PTR records when lease is deleted.
- Dynamically update DNS A and PTR records for DHCP clients that do not request updates.

The DNS registration settings for IPv6 clients are as follows:

- Enable DNS dynamic updates according to the settings below:
    - o Dynamically update DNS AAAA and PTR records only if requested by the DHCP clients.
    - o Always dynamically update DNS AAAA and PTR records.
- Discard AAAA and PTR records when lease is deleted.

Name Protection

Windows Server 2012 DHCP offers a feature called Name Protection. Name Protection helps prevent non-Windows systems from registering a domain name in DNS that was already registered by a Windows system. Name Protection is enabled from the DNS Tab of scope properties or server properties.

Note: You must have secure dynamic updates enabled for Name Protection to work properly.

DNSUPDATEPROXY

Windows DNS servers allow for dynamic registration. One of the functions that DHCP servers can perform for you is DNS registration. When a DHCP server serves out an IP address to a client, the DHCP server can then register the server name and the IP address with the DNS server. Windows Active Directory environments also allow for what is called secure dynamic updates. With these secure dynamic updates, changes can only be made to a DNS registration by the system that made the registration. This becomes a problem when you are using DHCP to do the registrations and you have multiple DHCP servers on the network. Once one DHCP server does a registration, another DHCP server will not be able to make any changes to the registration. The DNSUPDATEPROXY built-in group provides a solution for this issue. If you add all of your DHCP servers to the DNSUPDATEPROXY group, then they will be able to modify registrations made by each other.

NAP (Microsoft Network Policy Server)

NAP is Network Access Protection. NAP is used to protect against unidentified clients being able to connect to the DHCP server and get IP configuration information. The problem with NAP is that it does not provide full protection. It can prevent malicious users from getting an IP address from the DHCP server, but it cannot prevent users who manually configure an IP address from connecting to the network.

You have two options when you want to enable NAP. You can either enable it on all of your DHCP server scopes or you can leave it disabled on all scopes. The NAP protection in DHCP gets its client configuration information from a Network Policy Server or NPS. In some cases, the NPS may not be available. You have to decide what you want to do when this is the case. You have three options:

Full Access: This is the least secure option, but is the most flexible.
Restricted Access: This option tries to balance security and flexibility. But, it does require the maximum thought.
Drop Client Packet: This is the most secure option, but provides the least flexibility.

DNS

DNS is the Domain Name Service. It's used to map host names to IP addresses. It's hard to remember system IP addresses, especially when it comes to IPv6. So DNS can be very helpful. All you have to remember is the name, instead of the IP address. DNS can also be dangerous. DNS can be used to direct systems to malicious hosts. If all you know is the host name of a system, a DNS server might direct you to the IP address of a malicious host. When you are using a DNS for name resolution, there is an inherent trust between the client and the DNS server. The client trusts that the DNS server is sending it the correct IP address for the system that it is looking for. This trust can be exploited for malicious purposes.

DNS Overview

Before we get more into DNS, we should first talk a little about host names and host name resolution. The host name is simply the machine name assigned to the device. Usually when we think of a domain name, we are actually thinking about the fully qualified domain name. The fully qualified domain name, or FQDN, is the domain name along with a domain suffix. For example, the host name of a server may be server1, but the FQDN may be server1.company1.com.

Before DNS servers can be used, the clients in your environment must first be configured with the IP addresses of your DNS servers. This configuration can be done manually or through the use of DHCP. Since the client must be configured with the IP address of the DNS server, DNS is not considered to be totally anonymous process. There is some assurance that the DNS server a client is calling is who the client expects.

DNS Installation and Initial Configuration

1. On the Server Roles screen, as seen in Figure 2.14, select DNS Server. This will pop up the DNS Features window, as seen in Figure 2.15 which will warn you of mandatory features that must be installed with the DNS Server role. Click Add Features. This will take you back to the Server Roles screen. Verify that DNS Server is selected. Click Next.
2. Next is the Feature screen. Click Next.
3. Now you are presented with the DNS Server Information screen, as seen in Figure 2.16. Click Next.
4. Next is the Confirmation screen as seen in Figure 2.17. It tells you what roles and features will be installed. Click Install.
5. Next is the Results screen. You can view the progress, as seen in Figure 2.18.
6. Once the installation is complete, as seen in Figure 2.19, click Close.
7. Post-installation alert on dashboard.

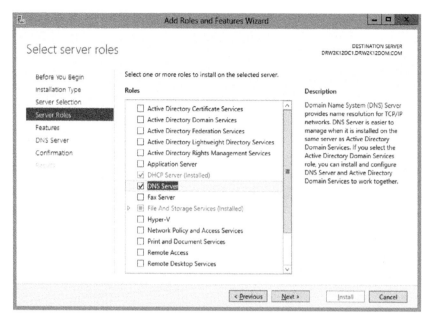

FIGURE 2.14 DNS Role

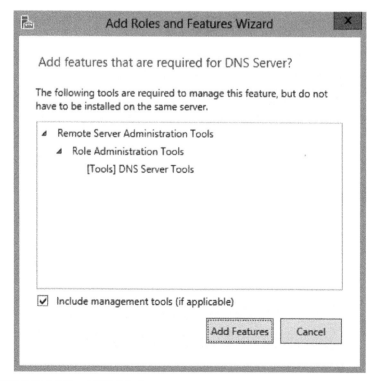

FIGURE 2.15 Additional DNS Role Features

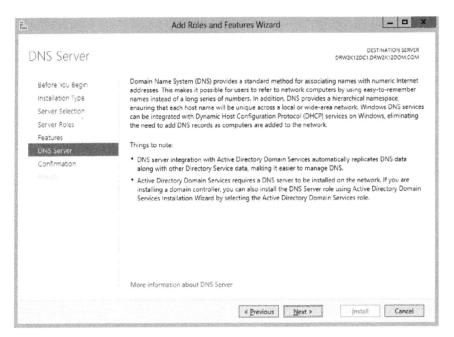

FIGURE 2.16 DNS Role Information Screen

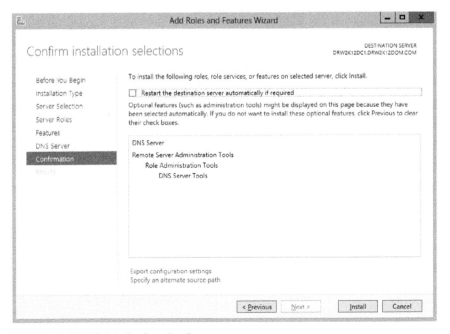

FIGURE 2.17 DNS Role Confirmation Screen

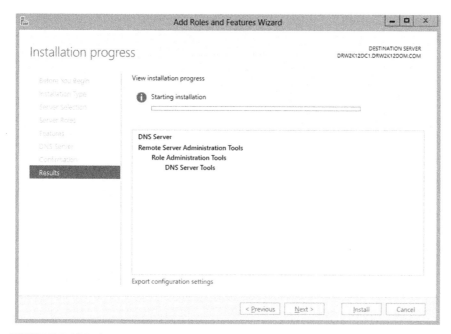

FIGURE 2.18 DNS Role Progress Screen

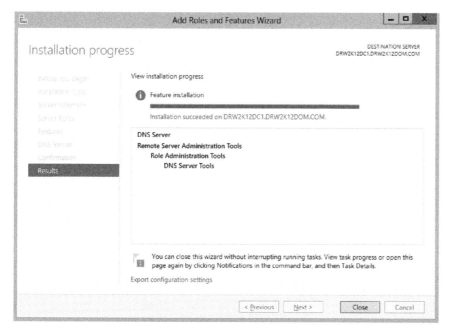

FIGURE 2.19 DNS Role Install Completion Screen

Creating Zones

There are two main categories of lookup zones: forward lookup zones and reverse lookup zones. Forward lookup zones are used to map a host name to an IP address. Reverse lookup zones are used to map IP addresses to host names.

Creating Forward Lookup Zones

Forward lookup zones hold name registrations for servers and services. They are the basis of what DNS servers do.

To create a forward lookup zone, perform the following steps:

1. Right-click on the Forward Lookup Zones folder, select New Zone. This will bring up the New Zone Wizard, as seen in Figure 2.20.
2. On the Welcome screen, click Next.
3. On the Zone Type screen, as seen in Figure 2.21, you choose what type of zone you are creating. You can choose Primary Zone, Secondary Zone, or Stub Zone. You also have the options to store the zone in Active Directory. Select Primary Zone, and click Next.
4. Next is the Zone Name screen, as seen in Figure 2.22. Here you must input the domain name for the DNS zone. Enter the name, and click Next.
5. Next you will see the Zone File screen, as seen in Figure 2.23. Here you can specify to create a new DNS zone file or use an existing one.

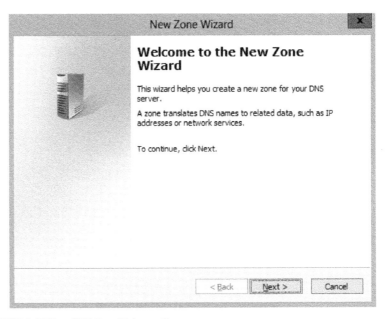

FIGURE 2.20 New DNS Zone Welcome Screen

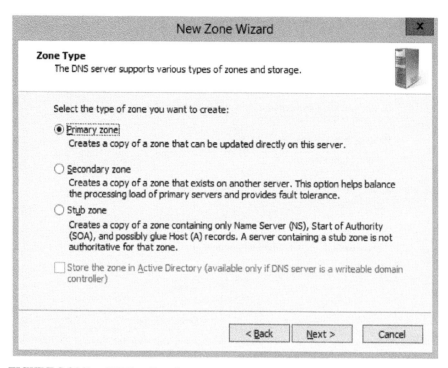

FIGURE 2.21 New DNS Zone Type Screen

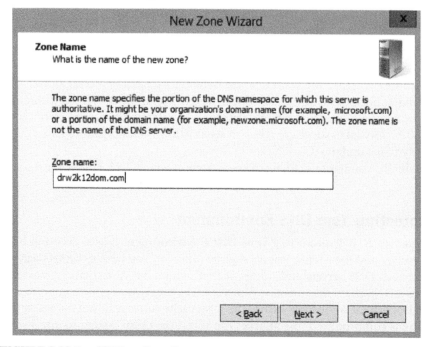

FIGURE 2.22 New DNS Zone Name Screen

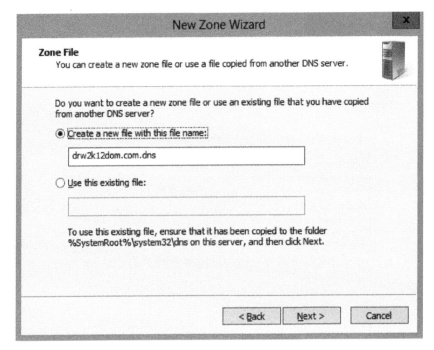

FIGURE 2.23 New DNS Zone File Screen

Since we are creating a new zone, we will choose to create a new zone file and click Next.

6. Next is the Dynamic Update screen, as seen in Figure 2.24. You must choose whether you want to allow dynamic updates. If you do allow dynamic updates, you must choose whether to allow unsecured dynamic updates or just secure dynamic updates. We plan to configure Active Directory later, so we are going to select Allow both nonsecure and secure dynamic updates. Click Next.

7. Finally, you have the final screen, as seen in Figure 2.25. Click Finish.

Protecting Your DNS Environment

Similar to DHCP, protecting your DHCP environment means securing both the server and the clients. But it's slightly different. You have to protect against malicious DNS servers and things of that nature. But, the client system contains a DNS client that must be protected. The main vulnerable component of the DNS client is the DNS cache. The DNS cache stores resolved names. If this cache is compromised, the attacker can direct the client system to any system they wish.

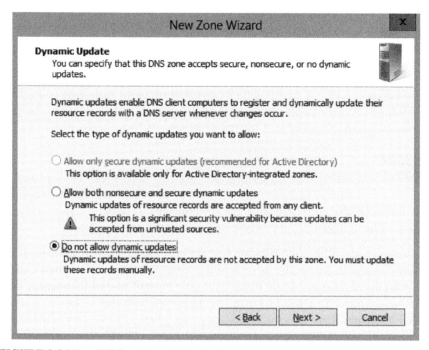

FIGURE 2.24 New DNS Zone Dynamic Update Screen

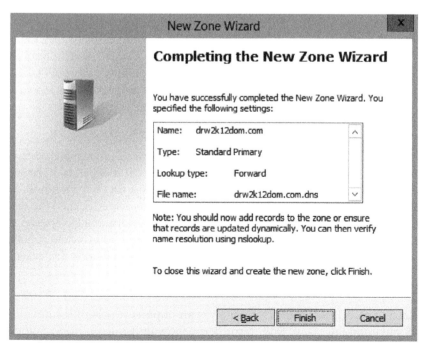

FIGURE 2.25 New DNS Zone Final Screen

Secure Cache Against Pollution

When a request is sent for a particular name record, the name server that was queried may respond with an NS record. Along with the NS record, there may also be an A record sent back that supposedly holds the IP address of the name server. This A record may not actually be valid. Without cache pollution protection disabled, that A record will be cached. With cache pollution protection enabled, the A record will not be cached. Instead a DNS lookup will be performed to get the IP address of the name server.

DNSSEC

DNSSEC is a set of extensions that are used to secure the DNS protocol. DNSSEC uses digital signatures to verify that the responses to DNS queries have not been altered. There are a few key concepts in DNSSEC. These include zone signing, authenticated denial-of-existence, and trust anchors:

- *Zone signing:* With zone signing, you are not just signing the zone itself; you are signing all of the records in the zone. Each record is signed individually. So, if changes are made, you only have to re-sign the records that were changed. You don't have to re-sign the whole zone.
- *Authenticated denial-of-existence:* Sometimes when a DNS query is made, there will not be any records to answer the query. In this case, there has to be a way for the client to know that the negative response from the DNS server is valid. The authenticated denial-of-existence provides a way for the DNS server to prove that the empty response is valid.
- *Trust anchors:* A trust is a public key that is associated with a DNS zone. A trust anchor allows a DNS server to validate DNSKEY resource records. On standalone DNS servers, trust anchors are stored in a file. On DNS servers running on domain controllers, the trust anchors can be stored in an Active Directory partition.

DNS Forwarders

DNS servers only hold records for a particular zone. So, what happens when the server receives a request for a zone that it does not hold? It depends on how the DNS server is configured. The server may just return an error saying it cannot find the record. But, if the DNS server is configured with a forwarder, then the server will forward the request to another DNS server. This additional DNS server can then answer the request. A DNS server can be configured so that certain zones are forwarded to certain servers or all zones may be forwarded to a particular server.

DNS Zone Security

Protecting your DNS zone information is an important part of securing your DNS environment. Your DNS records can provide valuable information as to the layout or configuration of your environment. There are other ways for attackers to get this information. But, you don't want to just hand it all over to them by allowing them access to all of your records.

SOA

All DNS zones have an SOA, or Start of Authority. This is the server that basically "owns" the records for the zone. The SOA is expected to be the master of record for the entries in a particular zone. It's important that the SOA is protected. You must be careful who is allowed access to this system.

DNS Zone Transfers

In addition to the primary DNS server for a zone, you may also have a secondary or other DNS servers. You need to have a way for the zone information to flow from the primary DNS server to the other DNS servers in the zone. This is done through zone transfers. A zone transfer allows you to transfer DNS information from one DNS server to another. You need to be careful when allowing zone transfers. You don't want to allow just any server to receive your zone information. You should limit which servers this information can be sent to.

To restrict zone transfers, perform the following steps:

1. Right-click on your desired zone, select properties.
2. Go to the Zone Transfers tab, as seen in Figure 2.26.

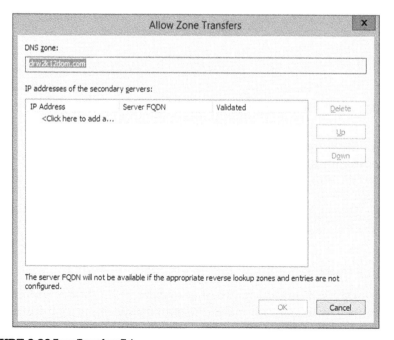

FIGURE 2.26 Zone Transfers Tab

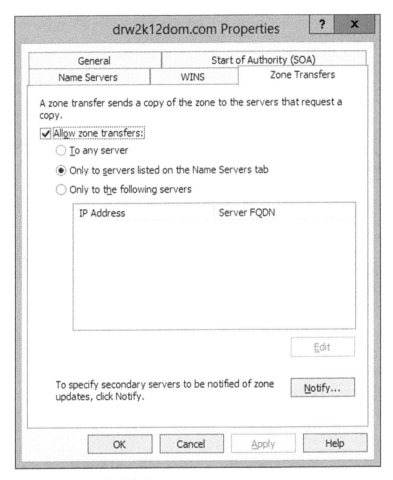

FIGURE 2.27 Allow Transfers Window

3. Select Allow zone transfers.
4. Choose Only to the following servers.
5. Click Edit. This will bring up the Allow Zone Transfers window, as seen in Figure 2.27.
6. Enter the name or IP address of the servers to which you would like to allow zone transfers. Click OK.

Dynamic Updates

Windows DNS servers allow for dynamic updates. This means the administrator does not have to manually make entries for the systems in a particular zone. The systems themselves can make the entries. This can be very convenient, but it can also pose a security risk. You have three options for dynamic updates:

Do not allow dynamic updates: This is the most secure option, but it will require all DNS entries to be manually added.

Allow dynamic updates: This is the most flexible option. But, it can pose a security risk.

Only allow secure dynamic updates: This option allows for the flexibility of dynamic updates, but it also checks permissions to ensure the system attempting to make the update actually has rights to make the update.

Note: Secure dynamic updates require that the zone be Active Directory integrated.

DNS Server Logging and Monitoring

An important part of securing your DNS environment is monitoring DNS activity. Not all malicious activity is overt. Monitoring and logging activity will help you find more subtle malicious activity. Monitoring and logging can also be used to determine if your DNS server is performing as expected.

Event Logging

Event logging allows you to view basic DNS activity. You can see information about name resolution requests, zone replication, and user activity. Event logging is enabled on the Event Logging tab of server properties, as seen in Figure 2.28. You can enable logging, for errors, warnings, or all activity.

Debug Logging

Debug logging offers more in-depth information about what's going on with your DNS server. You can see information about packets being sent and received by the DNS server. Debug logging is enabled on the Debug Logging tab of DNS server properties, as seen in Figure 2.29.

Monitoring

Monitoring is used to provide real-time information about what's going on with your DNS server. Monitoring is performed on the Monitoring tab of DNS serve properties, as seen in Figure 2.30. You can perform manual testing or automatic testing to find out if your server is functioning properly. You can choose to perform a simple query or a recursive query. The results will be displayed in the Test results window at the bottom of the page.

WINS

WINS is the Windows Internet Name Service. Similar to DNS, it's used to map Windows NetBIOS names to IP addresses. It's hard to remember system IP addresses, so WINS also can be very helpful. But, just like DNS, it can

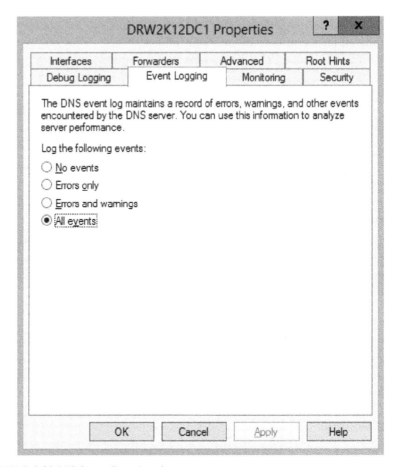

FIGURE 2.28 DNS Server Event Logging

also be dangerous. WINS can be used to direct systems to malicious hosts. WINS resolution requires the same trust between server and client that DNS requires.

Note: By default the IPv6 standard does not support NetBIOS; and therefore, does not support WINS.

WINS Overview

Windows systems can use a NetBIOS name to connect to each. It's a similar concept to the host name used with DNS. The main difference is that NetBIOS is not really an Internet standard. It's a Microsoft standard. Other operating

FIGURE 2.29 DNS Server Debug Logging

systems have added functionality to allow them to communicate via NetBIOS names, but NetBIOS is slowly being phased out.

WINS Feature Installation and Initial Configuration

1. On the Features Screen, as seen in Figure 2.31, select WINS Server. The wizard will pop up an additional features window, as seen in Figure 2.32. Click Add Features.
2. The Confirmation screen, as seen in Figure 2.33, will list all the features that will be installed with WINS. Click Install.
3. The Results screen will show you the progress of your WINS install. At the end of the installation, the Results window will let you know if the install was successful and if you received any errors or warnings.

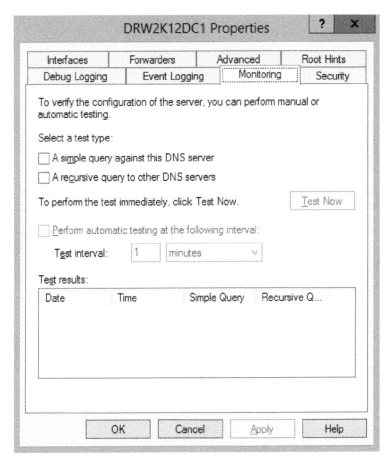

FIGURE 2.30 DNS Server Monitoring

Protecting Your WINS Environment

WINS is not only similar to DNS in the features that it provides, but it's also similar to DNS in the vulnerabilities that it has. You run the risk of both the client and the server being compromised.

WINS Server Database Verification

For the purpose of reliability and availability, WINS offers the ability to perform a database verification. It's basically a consistency check. You can verify the consistency of one WINS server database against another. You don't have to verify all of the records in the database, you can specify a maximum number to be checked. This can save you a lot of time if your WINS database is very large.

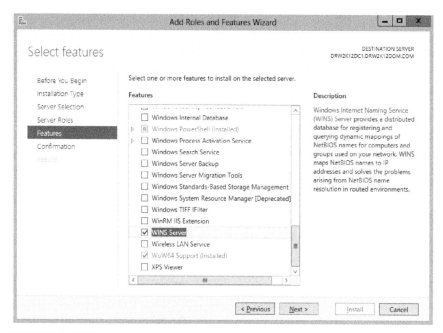

FIGURE 2.31 WINS Feature Installation

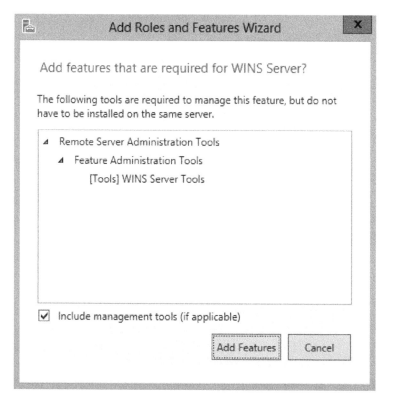

FIGURE 2.32 WINS Additional Features Window

Burst Handling

In order to ensure availability and prevent DOS attacks, WINS servers provide the ability to limit the amounts of registration requests that will be processed at once. It's called burst handling. You can go with predefined values or set your custom value. After the limit is reached, clients will be forced to retry their registration request.

WINS Server Logging

WINS allows you to enable detailed event logging. The information will be sent to the Windows Event Log. You must be careful when enabling detailed logging because of the performance degrading that can be caused.

WINS Replication

WINS Replication provides a means of fault tolerance for your WINS environment. WINS Replication is configured under the Replication Partners node, as seen in Figure 2.34. You can have multiple WINS servers in your environment and keep these servers in sync using replication. There are two types of WINS replication available: push replication and pull replication. You can specify when to start the replication and how often to repeat it. Replication can be used to ensure consistency, but it also takes resources to perform. You will have to determine the schedule that is best for your organization. To ensure the integrity of replication, you can also specify who your WINS servers are allowed to replicate with and what types of records can be overwritten. To configure replication options, you configure the properties for your replication partners as seen in Figure 2.35.

FIGURE 2.33 WINS Confirmation

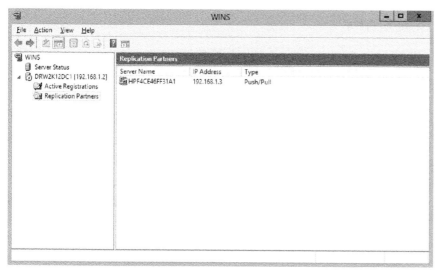

FIGURE 2.34 WINS Replication Partners

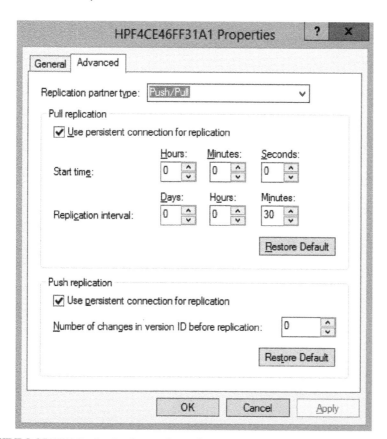

FIGURE 2.35 WINS Replication Partner Properties

SUMMARY

Securing your infrastructure is crucial to securing your network. Your DHCP, DNS, and WINS infrastructure provide networking services throughout your network. Protecting these services is critical.

DHCP provides IP addressing services for your network. You can use DHCP to automatically configure clients with IP addresses, DNS Server address, and other important information. You have to ensure you secure the client side and the server side of your DHCP environment.

DNS provides name resolution services for your environment. A compromised DNS environment can be used to direct clients to malicious sites. There are several security measures you can use to ensure the integrity of your DNS environment and to protect your servers.

WINS is used for NetBIOS resolution for IPv4 clients. It operates similarly to DNS and has many of the same potential issues as DNS. The usage of WINS has diminished in many environments, but it's still important that you secure your WINS environment.

CHAPTER 3

Securing Network Access

INFORMATION IN THIS CHAPTER

- General Network Settings
- Wireless Security
- Windows Firewall
- IPSec
- Windows 8 Resource Sharing
- Windows Server 2012 Resource Sharing

CONTENTS

INTRODUCTION

Now that your infrastructure is in place, you can begin configuring your other systems. When configuring your systems, you can choose to take the easy route, or the more secure route. Although, Windows has a lot of configuration options that are secured by default, there are others where you must choose the secure option.

Resource sharing is an important part of network access. Securing resource sharing will protect clients and servers from malicious activity. We will go over securing resource access in Windows 8 and Windows Server 2012.

GENERAL NETWORK SETTINGS

There are some basic network configuration settings that will apply no matter the connection method. These settings affect the overall security of the system. So it's important that you understand them and set them correctly.

Network Discovery

Network discovery is what allows computers and other devices to be discovered on a network. With network discovery, a system will send out messages over the network looking for devices that are discoverable. Having network discovery enabled makes it easy for you to share network resources between the systems you want. But, it also makes it easier for an attacker to find these resources. Because of this, you might want network discovery turned on for some systems and off for other systems. For network discovery to be fully functional, the following must be in place: the DNS client enabled on the system doing the discovery, SSDP discovery, Function Discovery Resource Publication, and the UPnP Device Host service must be started.

Network Location

When configuring your network settings, when you attempt to connect to a network for the first time, you are prompted for a network location. Although network locations are selected when you first connect to a network, you can also change the network location later. Network locations are used to apply a preset list of settings for that particular network. There are four network locations that can be used: home, work, public, and domain.

Home Network

This option is for computers connected to a home network. This is the most trusted network option. By default, network discovery is turned on for Home networks. Selecting the home network will enable the HomeGroup option.

Work Network

This option is for computers connected to the network at your workplace. Generally this option is for smaller networks; networks where computers generally exist in a workgroup or no real network grouping at all. Network discovery will be turned on by default. The HomeGroup option will not be enabled for work networks.

Public Network

This option if for computers connected to a public, untrusted network. This is considered to be the least trust of the network locations. The rest of the computers on the network is generally unknown to you and you do not want them to be able to access your system resources or devices. Because of this, network discovery will be turned off by default. There will also be no option to enable a HomeGroup.

Domain Network

The fourth option is a domain network. This option actually cannot be chosen. If you are on a corporate network, your domain administrator must choose to enable this option. If the domain administrator chooses this option, the user is unable to change it. It must be changed by the administrator.

WIRELESS SECURITY

When configuring your wireless networks, you have a few security-related choices to make. You have to know what settings are required for a desired network. You also have to decide whether or not you want to connect a particular based on the security settings in place. These settings can help secure wireless networks, although some people would argue that there is no real way to protect wireless networks because they are inherently insecure.

Wireless Properties

Wireless connections have a few general properties that must be configured. Two of which are of specific security concern.

Connect Automatically When This Network is in Range

This option is considered to be one mostly of convenience. Users don't always have to manually connect to a wireless network when the system starts up. But, it can present a security issue. When a system is set to automatically connect to a wireless network, there is an increased chance that the system will connect to a rogue access point.

Connect Even If the Network is Not Broadcasting
Its Name (SSID)

As a security measure, administrators often prevent their wireless networks from broadcasting the SSID. This doesn't prevent malicious users from connecting, but it can make it slightly more difficult. When a network is not broadcasting the SSID, your Windows system will not connect to it unless this option is enabled.

Security Types

When connecting to a wireless network, you first have to know what security type is used. You can think of the security type as basically the authentication method. You have several options to choose from: including Open, 802.1x, WPA, and WPA2.

As you probably figured, the Open option does not enable any type of authentication. In turn, it is the least secure option available. It should not be used on networks where sensitive data reside. The reason you may use this option is if you want to provide guest access. It would be highly recommended that you segment off this network from the rest of your network. But, you should make sure you realize that anyone can access this network.

802.1x authentication can use a central authentication server for authentication. It allows for advanced authentication methods like smart cards.

Shared enables a shared key authentication system. In this system, a predefined key is created. This key is used to secure the wireless network. In order to secure the network, the client system must be configured with this key.

WPA is WiFi Protected Access. WPA-Personal uses a preshared key for authentication. WPA-Enterprise uses a central authentication server for authenticating connections. WPA2 was developed in 2004 as an enhancement to the original standard. It was done to fix some of the security issues in the first standard and to add additional features.

Wireless Encryption

Once you have made a connection to a wireless network, you then have to worry about protecting the data transmissions. This is generally done through wireless encryption. There are three main encryption types available now in Windows: WEP, TKIP, and AES.

WEP

WEP stands for Wired Equivalent Privacy. It's one of the original encryption methods used for wireless connections. Since its initial introduction, WEP has been found to be somewhat insecure. There have been instances where WEP encryption has been broken. Because of this, people are moving away from it whenever possible.

TKIP

TKIP is the Temporal Key Integrity Protocol. TKIP was originally intended to be an upgraded replacement for WEP. But, the problem is that TKIP uses similar encryption mechanisms as WEP. Because of this, the security of the protocol comes into question.

AES

AES is the Advanced Encryption Standard. AES is considered to be much stronger that previous encryption methods. AES allows for up to 256-bit keys. It is the preferred method of wireless encryption. AES is currently the encryption standard for federal government use. It's also acceptable for use in a FIPS compliant environment.

Table 3.1 Wireless Security and Encryption Types

Security Type	Encryption Type
No authentication	WEP
WPA2-Personal	AES and TKIP
WPA-Personal	AES and TKIP
WPA2-Enteprise	AES and TKIP
WPA-Enterprise	AES and TKIP
802.1x	WEP

Security and Encryption Types

For wireless connections, there are a number of security types and encryption types available. Table 3.1 shows the options available.

WINDOWS FIREWALL

Windows Firewall, as seen in Figure 3.1, not only protects your system's Internet connections, but also protects all network connections. The initial Windows Firewall screen is largely a status screen. When you first open Windows Firewall, you will see the status of your current network location, as seen in Figure 3.1. You will see the Windows Firewall state; whether it's on or off. You can also see the status of incoming connections. You can see the active networks and the notification state.

If you have Windows Firewall turned off, there is an option for **Use recommended settings**. This option will set all the recommended configuration settings for your system. Before you choose this option, you can check to see what configuration setting changes will be made.

Network Profiles

Windows Firewall configuration is based on network types, called profiles. There are three profiles available for configuration:

Guest or public networks: This profile is used when the system is connected to public network, such as airport or coffee shop. In this case you want to set very restrictive access because you shouldn't trust the other systems on the network.

Private networks: This profile is used when the system is connected to a home or work network, in workgroup mode. In this case, the other systems on the network are generally trusted to some degree.

Domain networks: This profile is used for networks connected to an Active Directory domain. In this case, settings are often controlled by group policy.

FIGURE 3.1 Windows Firewall

Network Profile Information

Windows Firewall displays basic status information for each network profile. You will be able to see which network profile is currently in use (displayed as Connected vs. Not Connected). You will also see the following information:

Windows Firewall state: This option will let you know if Windows Firewall is on or off for the given network type.

Incoming connections: This option will tell you the current policy in place for connections. You might see Block all connections to apps that are not on the list of allowed apps or Block all connections including apps on the list of allowed apps.

Active <profile type> networks: This option shows the network(s) that you are currently connected to.

Notification state: This option details what notifications have been configured for Windows Firewall.

Note: If you have multiple physical adapters or using virtualization, you may show as being connected to multiple networks simultaneously.

Windows Firewall Configuration

If you want to make changes to Windows Firewall, other than setting the recommended settings, you have to use the options on the right-hand side of the screen. They are Allow a program or feature through Windows Firewall, Change notification settings, Turn Windows Firewall on or off, Restore defaults, Advanced settings, and Troubleshoot my network.

Allow an App or Feature Through Windows Firewall

Many network-based applications will not run properly if they are not enabled through the firewall. Choosing the option **Allow a program or feature through Windows Firewall** will bring up the Allowed apps window, as seen in Figure 3.2. Here, you can choose which programs will be allowed to

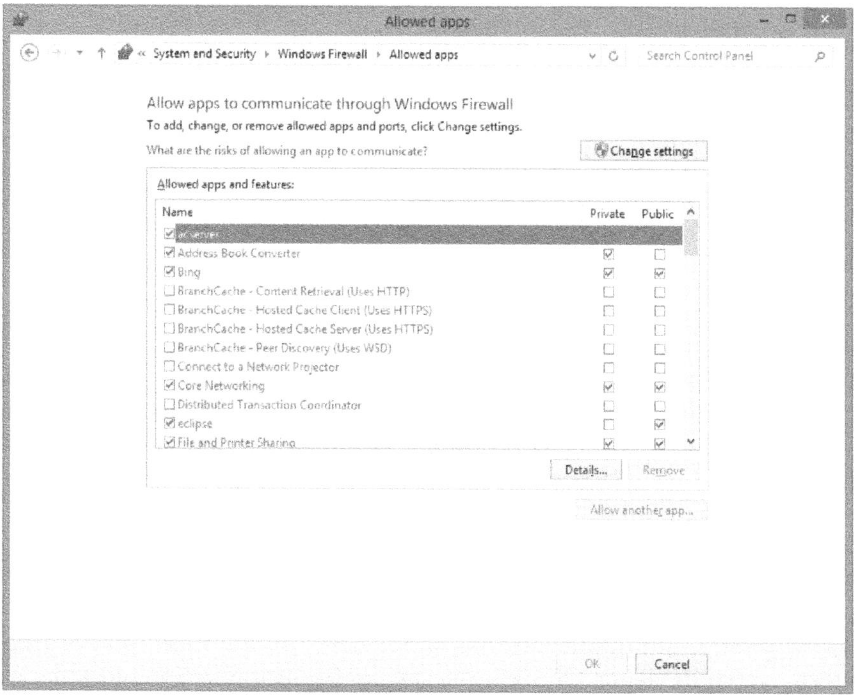

FIGURE 3.2 Windows Firewall Allowed Apps

FIGURE 3.3 Windows Firewall Edit an App Window

move through the firewall. You can choose which network the program will be allowed to communicate on. You can choose either Private or Public.

Note: You have to select the Change settings option in order to be able to make any changes on the Allowed apps screen.

If you click the Details button, this will bring up the **Edit an app** window as seen in Figure 3.3. Here you can view detailed information for an application. You will be able to see the actual executable that is configured for the application. You can also change the network types that have been selected for the application.

If you want to remove an application from the list, click the Remove button. You will be asked to confirm that you want to remove the application from the list. Just click Yes and you're done.

There is a default list of programs provided for you, but if you would like to allow a program that you don't see, you can choose **Allow another app**. This will bring up the Add an app window as seen in Figure 3.4. Here you must specify the path to the application you would like to add. You also choose which network you want the application to be allowed on. After you are finished, just click the Add button and your application will be added to the list.

Change Notification Settings

Windows Firewall can be configured to not only block networks connections, but also to give notifications when an application may be blocked. If you choose Change notification settings, it will bring up the Customize Settings screen as seen in Figure 3.5. Here you can configure application blocking settings and enable notifications for when an application is blocked.

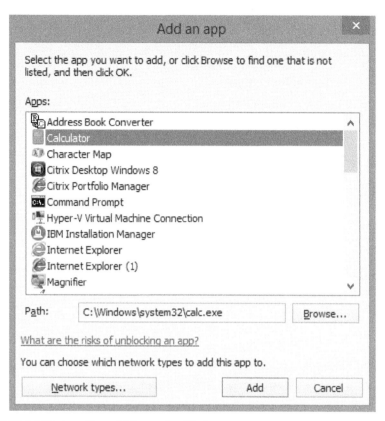

FIGURE 3.4 Windows Firewall Allow an App Window

Turn Windows Firewall On or Off
Selecting Turn Windows Firewall on or off will bring up the Customize Settings screen. Here you can enable or disable Windows Firewall for a particular network type.

Restore Defaults
Selecting Restore defaults will bring up the Restore defaults screen as seen in Figure 3.6. If you click the Restore defaults button, it will reset your Windows Firewall configuration back to defaults.

Windows Firewall with Advanced Security
Selecting Advanced settings will bring up the Windows Firewall with Advanced Security application. Here you have much more granular control over your Windows Firewall rules.

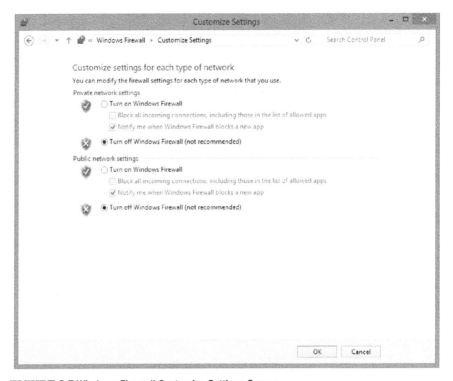

FIGURE 3.5 Windows Firewall Customize Settings Screen

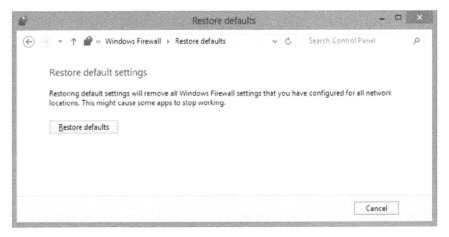

FIGURE 3.6 Windows Firewall Restore Defaults Screen

Inbound Rules

The Inbound Rules section, as seen in Figure 3.7, will include a listing of all the configured inbound rules on system. From here, you can also see general

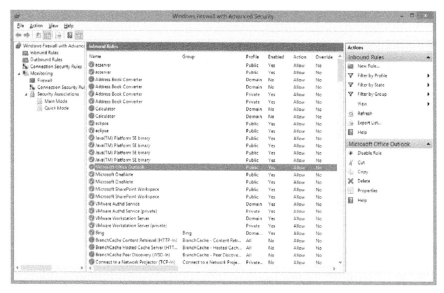

FIGURE 3.7 Windows Firewall Inbound Rules

information for each rule, such as name, program, local address, remote address, and authorized users. A gray check will denote that the rule is disabled. A green[1] check will denote that the rule is enabled.

Windows Firewall Rule Properties

If you double-click on a rule or right-click and select Properties, you can view detailed properties for each rule. These detailed properties allow you more fine-grained control over each rule. You can enable or disable a rule. You can also set restrictions on client systems and remote users. When you view rule properties, there are eight tabs available: General, Programs and Services, Remote Computers, Protocols and Ports, Scope, Advanced, Local Principals, and Remote Users.

General

The General tab, as seen in Figure 3.8, will provide you with basic information about the rule like the name and the description. You will be able to see if the rule is enabled or not.

Here, you can also configure what action will be taken when a connection matches the rule. You can choose to block the connection, allow the connection, or to allow the connection if it is secure. If you select the Allow the

---

[1] For interpretation of color in Figure 3.7, the reader is referred to the web version of this book.

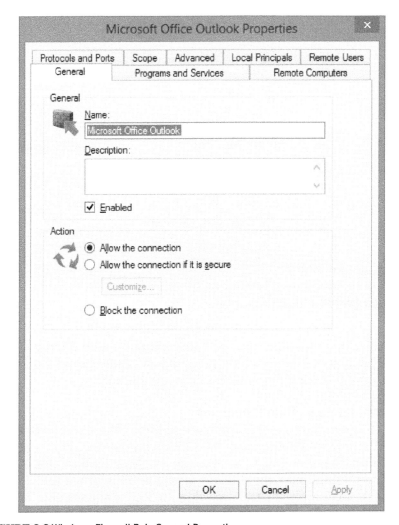

FIGURE 3.8 Windows Firewall Rule General Properties

connection if it is secure option and click the Customize button, it will bring up the Customize Allow if Secure Settings window, as seen in Figure 3.9. You have four options to choose from:

- *Allow the connection if it is authenticated and integrity-protected:* This option requires the use of IPSec.
- *Require the connection to be encrypted:* This option is used to force encryption on a connection. You can also allow encryption to be dynamically negotiated, which means packets can still be sent while encryption is being negotiated.

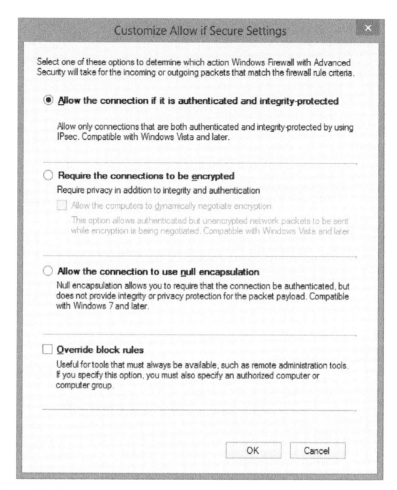

FIGURE 3.9 Windows Firewall Customize Allow If Secure Settings

- *Allow connection to use null encapsulation:* With null encryption, the connection is authenticated but the payload is not protected.
- *Override block rules:* This setting is used to ensure that the connection will always be allowed. This will help prevent you from unintentionally blocking a connection.

Programs and Services

The Programs and Services tab, as seen in Figure 3.10, allows you to specify to which programs and/or services this rule will apply. In the Programs section, you can choose to apply the rule to a specific program or all programs that meet specific conditions.

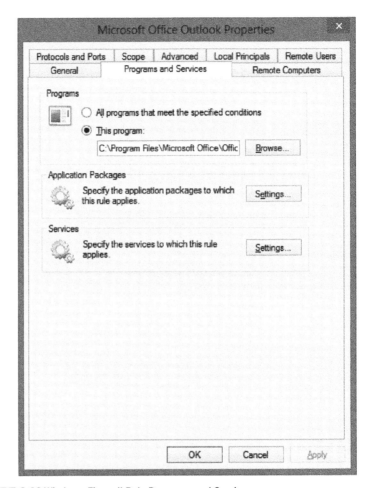

FIGURE 3.10 Windows Firewall Rule Programs and Services

If you click on Settings in the Application Packages section, it will bring up the Custom Application Package Settings window, as seen in Figure 3.11. Here you specify if you want the rule to apply to all programs and application packages, only to application packages, or a specific application package.

If you click on Settings in the Services section, it will bring up the Custom Service Settings window, as seen in Figure 3.12. Here you specify if you want the rule to apply to all programs and services, only to services, or to a specific service.

Remote Computers

The Remote Computers tab, as seen in Figure 3.13, allows you to set up computer-specific conditions. You can choose to only allow connections from a list of specific computers or to skip the rule for a list of specific computers.

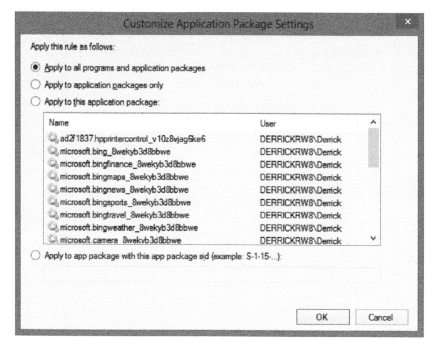

FIGURE 3.11 Windows Firewall Custom Application Package Settings

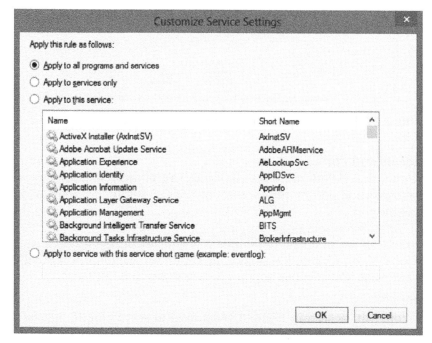

FIGURE 3.12 Windows Firewall Custom Service Settings

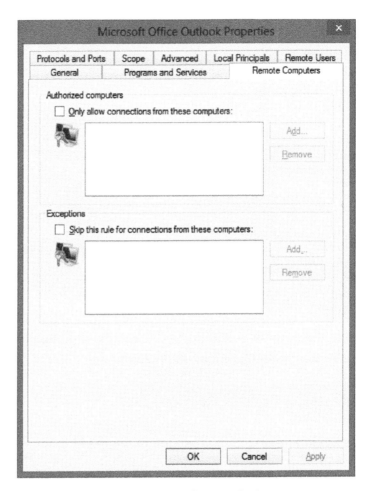

FIGURE 3.13 Windows Firewall Rule Remote Computer Settings

Protocols and Ports

The Protocols and Ports tab, as seen in Figure 3.14, allows you to specify a specific protocol and port for the connection. You can specify the local port and the remote port.

If you select ICMP as the protocol, then you will have the option to configure additional ICMP settings. If you click the Customize button, it will bring up the Customize ICMP Settings window as seen in Figure 3.15.

Scope

The Scope tab, as seen in Figure 3.16, is used to specify the IP address or addresses that the rule will apply to. You can specify a specific IP address, a subnet, or an IP address range.

FIGURE 3.14 Windows Firewall Rule Protocols and Ports

Advanced

The Advanced tab, as seen in Figure 3.17, allows you to configure which network profile(s) (domain, private, or public) the rule will apply to. You can also specify which interface types (local area network, remote access, or wireless) the rule will apply to. Finally you can configure edge traversal which will determine what to do with unsolicited traffic that has passed through a NAT router or firewall.

Local Principals

The Local Principals tab, as seen in Figure 3.18, is used to specify local users for whom the rule will apply. You can specify a list user for only whom connections

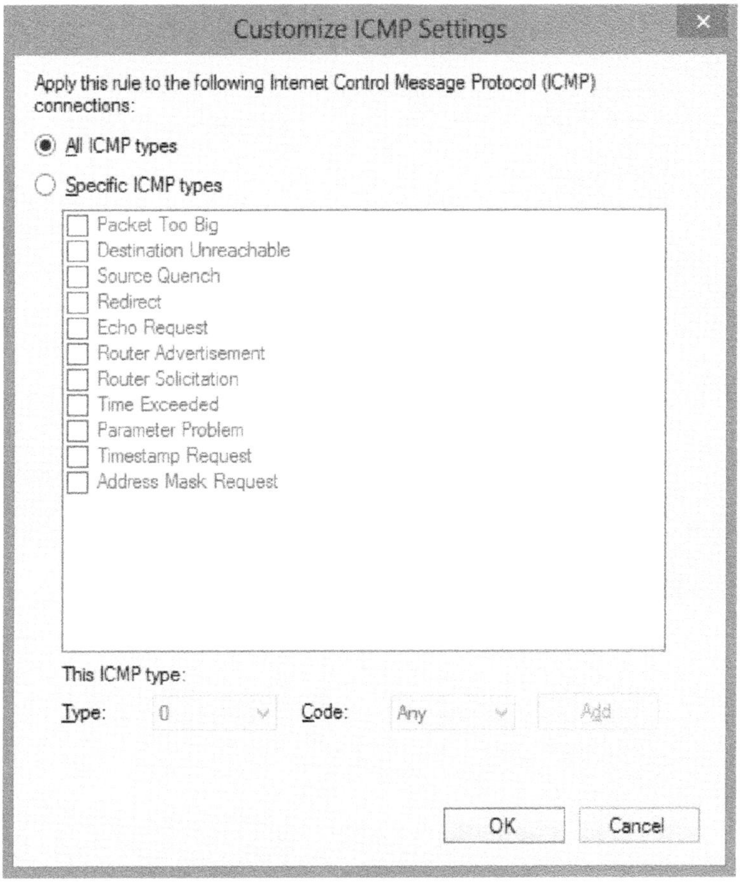

FIGURE 3.15 Windows Firewall Rule ICMP Settings

will be allowed. You can also specify a list of users for whom the rule will be skipped.

Remote Users

The Remote Users tab, as seen in Figure 3.19, is used to specify remote users for whom the rule will apply. You can specify a list of users for whom only connections will be allowed. You can also specify a list of users for whom the rule will be skipped.

Outbound Rules

The Outbound Rules section is very similar to the Inbound Rules section. If you double-click on a rule or right-click and select Properties, you can view detailed properties for each rule. These detailed properties allow you more fine-grained

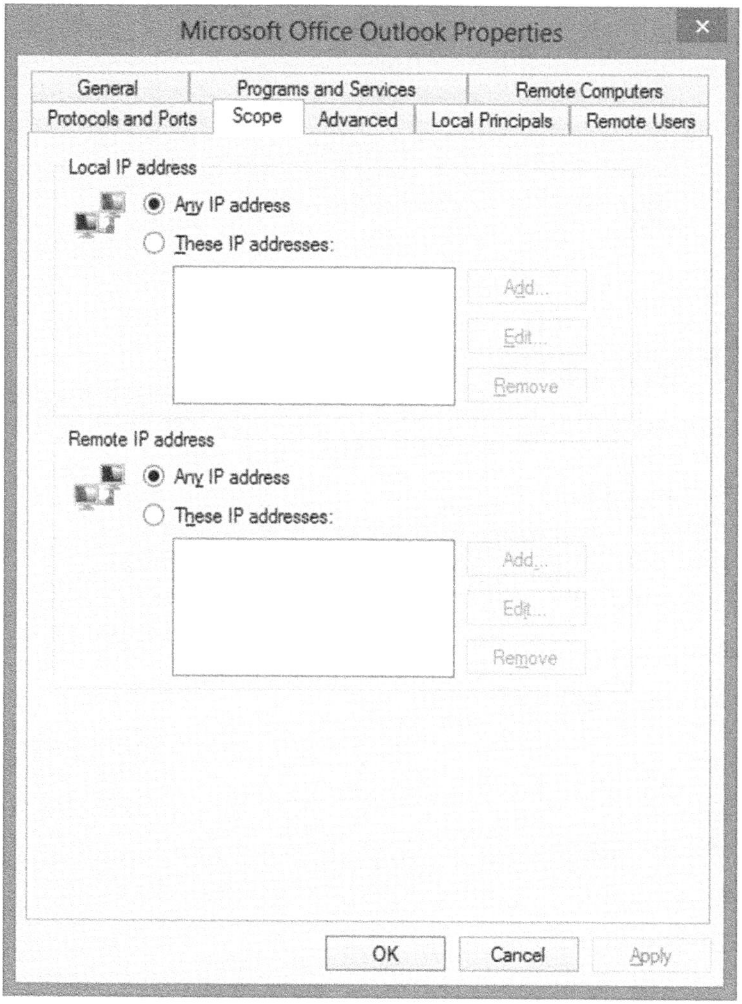

FIGURE 3.16 Windows Firewall Rule Scope

control over each rule. The properties available for outbound rules are slightly different than the properties available for inbound rules. The two most noticeable changes are on the lack of a Remote Users tab, and the lack of the Edge traversal section on the Advanced tab.

Monitoring

The Monitoring section is used to monitor firewall and IPSec activity on your system. There are three nodes in the Monitoring section: Firewall, Connection Security Rules, and Security Associations. We will cover Connection Security Rules and Security Associations in the IPSec of the chapter.

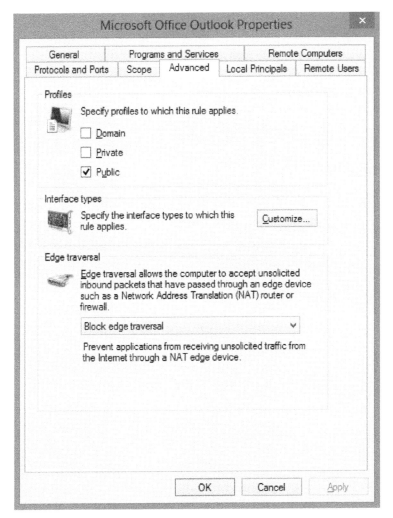

FIGURE 3.17 Windows Firewall Rule Advanced Properties

Firewall

The Firewall section under Monitoring, as seen in Figure 3.20, will show you information about the active inbound firewall rules on your system. You can see information like the rule name, the profile, local and remote addresses, and much more.

IPSEC

IPSec is short for Internet Protocol Security. We could spend all day going over IPSec. But, for this book we'll just give a brief overview, then get into how it's used and configured in Windows systems.

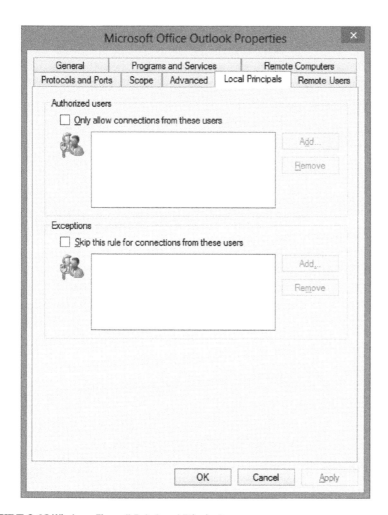

FIGURE 3.18 Windows Firewall Rule Local Principals

IPSec Overview

IPSec is used for securing IP communications. IPSec has three deployment models: network-to-network, host-to-host, and host-to-network. The one we will be concerned with here is host-to-host; because that's the deployment model generally used with individual Windows systems. IPSec consists of three main implementations IPSec AH, IPSec ESP, and IPSec Security Associations. Each of these serves a different purpose and has different benefits.

IPSec AH

AH is the Authentication Headers form of IPSec. IPSec AH is used to secure the headers in an IP packet. It's also used to authenticate packets so that you know

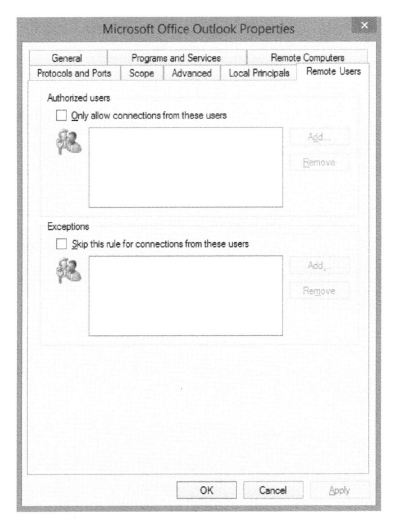

FIGURE 3.19 Windows Firewall Rule Remote Users

they are coming from a verified source. Since packet headers are authenticated, IPSec AH can also help protect against replay attacks.

IPSec ESP

ESP is the Encapsulated Security Payload form of IPSec. IPSec ESP is used to secure the data within an IP packet. This data is also called the payload. IPSec ESP is often used when confidentiality is a concern. Malicious attackers will not be able to read the data in a packet, if it's secured using IPSec ESP.

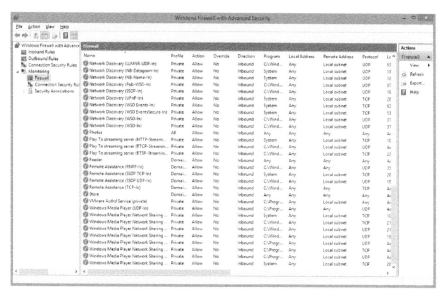

FIGURE 3.20 Windows Firewall—Firewall Monitoring

IPSec Security Associations

Security associations are pairs used to authenticate and encrypt network flows. Security associations allow for varied means of protection to be used for different flows and packets.

Configuring IPSec

IPSec is configured inside Windows Firewall. Choosing Advanced settings in Windows Firewall will bring up the Windows Firewall with Advanced Security application. Here, you have the Connection Security Rules plug-in that can be used to configured IPSec.

You can create isolation, authentication exemption, server-to-server, tunnel, and custom rules:

- Isolation rules can be used to restrict connections based on authentication.
- Authentication exemption rules allow you to make connections to certain computers without the connection having to be authenticated.
- Server-to-server rules are used to authenticate connections between specific computers.
- Tunnel rules are also used to authenticate connections between two computers.
- Custom rules.

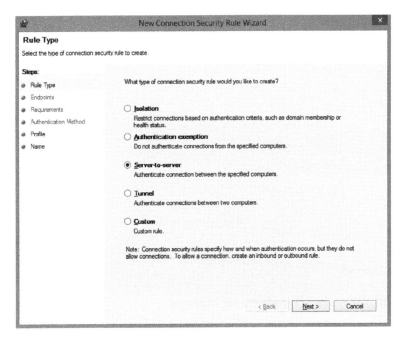

FIGURE 3.21 Windows Firewall New Connection Security Rule Type Screen

Creating a Server-to-Server IPSec Connection Rule

Right-clicking on Connection Security Rules and selecting New Rule will bring up the Rule Type screen of the New Connection Security Rule Wizard, as seen in Figure 3.21. Here you decide what type of connection rule you want to create. Select Server-to-server. Click Next.

This will bring up the Endpoints screen, as seen in Figure 3.22. Here you specify which endpoint systems will have their communication secured. Add the endpoints you want secured and click Next.

This will bring up the Requirements screen, as seen in Figure 3.23. This is where you specify the conditions where the rule be applied. You can choose between three options:

- *Request authentication for inbound and outbound connections:* With this option, authentication is requested but not required.
- *Require authentication for inbound connections and request authentication for outbound connections:* Inbound connections must use authentication. Outbound connections request authentication, but it is not required.
- *Require authentication for inbound and outbound connections:* Inbound and outbound connections must use authentication.

Choose your desired option and click Next.

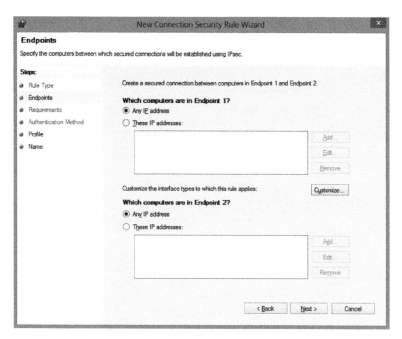

FIGURE 3.22 Windows Firewall New Connection Security Rule Endpoints Screen

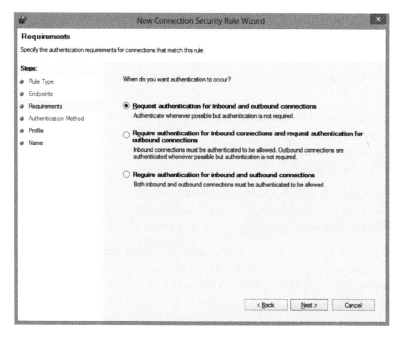

FIGURE 3.23 Windows Firewall New Connection Security Rule Requirements Screen

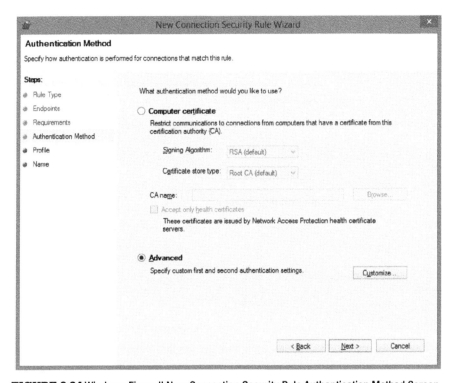

FIGURE 3.24 Windows Firewall New Connection Security Rule Authentication Method Screen

This brings up the Authentication method screen, as seen in Figure 3.24. You can choose to either use a computer certificate for authentication or choose a custom method.

If you choose Computer Certificate, all computers must have certificates issued by the designated certificate authority. You also have the option to require health certificates. Health certificates are issued by Network Access Protection health certificate servers.

If you select the Advanced option, you have to specify at one custom authentication method. Clicking the Customize button, will bring up the Customize Advanced Authentication Methods screen as seen in Figure 3.25.

Here you can set up a first and a second authentication method. You can configure multiple authentication methods for the each. If you select Add under First authentication, you will see the Add First Authentication Method window as seen in Figure 3.26.

You can choose to authenticate using Kerberos v5, NTLMv2, a computer certificate, or a preshared key. If you choose the computer certificate option, you

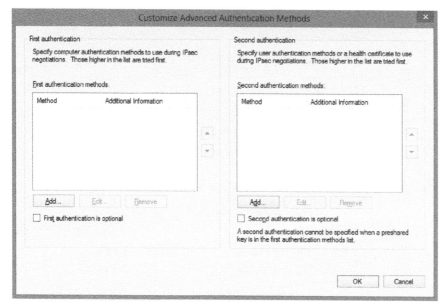

FIGURE 3.25 Windows Firewall New Connection Security Rule Custom Authentication Method Screen

must select the certificate authority that the computer certificates must have been issued from. If you choose the computer certificate option, you also have the option to configure advanced properties. Clicking the Advanced button, will bring up the Advanced Certificate Criteria Properties window, as seen in Figure 3.27.

Here you can specify additional restrictions on the certificate. You specify a specific key usage that must be specified in the certificate. You can also configure certain name values, like a subject OU that must be used in the certificate. These additional settings are particularly useful if you specified a public CA. You have no control over who can receive certificates from a public CA, so being able to add further restrictions is a good way to enhance security.

Note: Caution should be used when selecting preshared key as the authentication method. Preshared keys are stored in plaintext; and therefore are subject to theft.

Next is the Profile screen as seen in Figure 3.28. Here you specify the network type(s) for which you want the rule to apply. Your choices are Domain, Private, and Public.

Finally, you must give your new security rule a name. You can also add an optional description if you like.

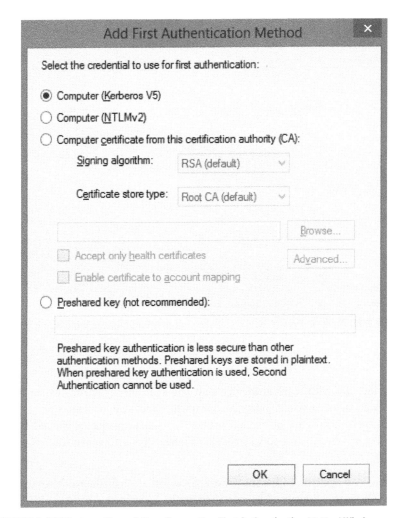

FIGURE 3.26 Windows Firewall New Connection First Authentication Method Window

Note: Inbound and Outbound firewall rules must still be configured in order to use IPSec. IPSec will secure the connection, but it must first be allowed through the firewall.

IPSec Monitoring in Windows Firewall with Advanced Security

IPSec monitoring can be done in the Monitoring section of Windows Firewall with Advanced Security. There are two nodes that will provide you the information you need: Connection Security Rules and Security Associations.

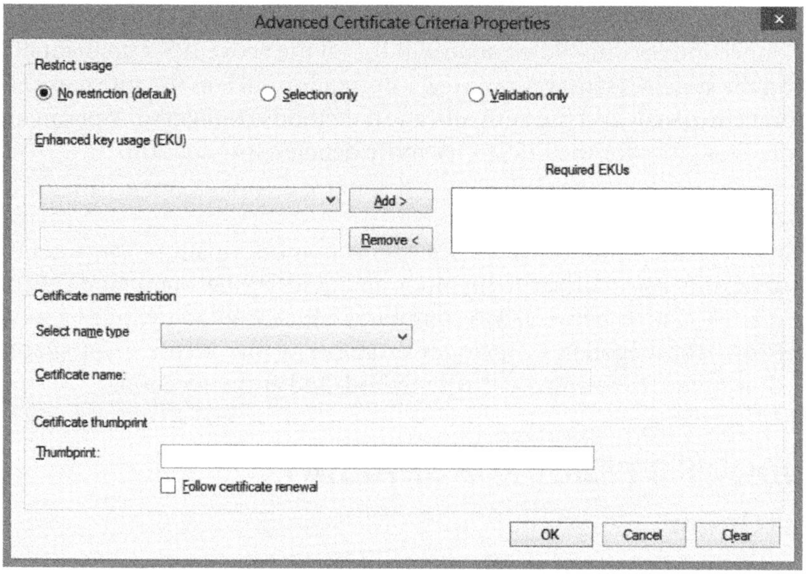

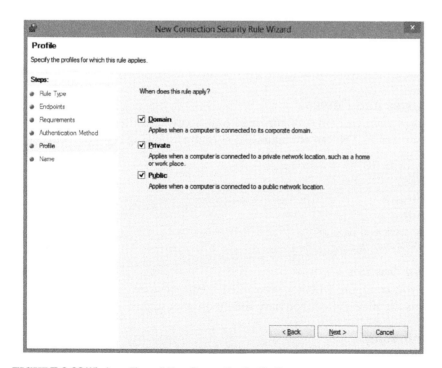

FIGURE 3.27 Windows Firewall New Connection Advanced Certificate Criteria Properties Window

FIGURE 3.28 Windows Firewall New Connection Profile Screen

Connection Security Rules

The Connection Security Rules node will list all the active IPSec configuration rules on the system. Here you can view information such as the rule name, the endpoints involved, and the authentication methods configured. You can also view the properties for the rule, to see more detailed information.

Security Associations

Security associations are stored secure connection information. There are two types of security associations: main mode and quick mode. Main mode negotiation is a negotiation between two computers which want to establish a secure connection. The negotiation includes establishing the secure cryptographic protection suite, determining the key method, and authentication.

WINDOWS 8 RESOURCE SHARING

HomeGroup

The concept of a computer workgroup has been a part of the Windows world for a long time. In recent years, Windows has introduced the concept of a HomeGroup. Workgroups and HomeGroups follow a very similar concept. A HomeGroup is a group of computers on your home network that are allowed to share resources. Because of the access allowed to members of a HomeGroup, you should set a secure password for your HomeGroup.

You HomeGroup can be configured under PC settings. If you have not enabled a HomeGroup, you will be given the option to do so, as seen in Figure 3.29.

Libraries and Devices

In this section, you can configure read-only access to content you have shared on your system. You can configure access to the following types of content:

- Documents.
- Music.
- Pictures.
- Videos.
- Printers and devices.

Media Devices

Here you configure whether networked media devices like TVs and gaming systems can play content you have shared on your system.

Membership

Under the membership section, you can perform two tasks. First, you can configure a password for the HomeGroup. If others want to join the HomeGroup,

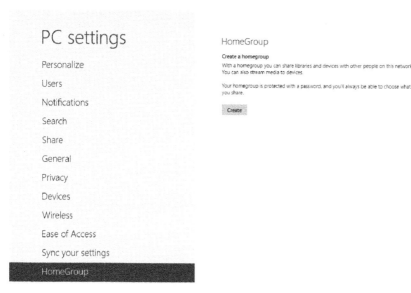

FIGURE 3.29 Create HomeGroup Screen

they will have to enter this password. Second, you can choose to leave the HomeGroup. If you leave the HomeGroup, you will no longer have access to shared resources.

Advanced Sharing Settings

The advanced sharing settings window, as seen in Figure 3.30, will allow you to configure more granular settings for device sharing. The configuration options here are split into three categories. These categories denote different types of network connections that would generally have different risk levels and therefore different security settings. The three options available are Private, Guest or Public, and All Networks. When you enter the advanced sharing settings configuration window, it will show which is your current profile.

There are several options here that you need to be aware. Each network profile has different default settings.

Private

The Private profile, as seen in Figure 3.31, is generally for trusted networks like home networks. The first option is network discovery. Network discovery determines whether your computer can discover other devices on the network. It also determines whether or not your computer can be discovered by other computers. The first decision you must make is whether or not you want

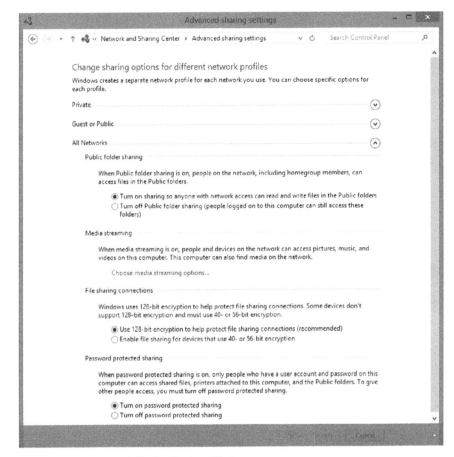

FIGURE 3.30 Advanced Sharing Settings Window

network discovery to be turned on. If it is turned on, then you must decide if you want to enable automatic setup of network connected devices. The default options are **Turn on network discovery** and **Turn on automatic setup of network devices**.

The next option is file and printer sharing. File and printer sharing must be enabled for you to be able to share files and devices on your computer with other users on the network. You have two options here. You can either choose **Turn on file and printer sharing** or **Turn off file and printer sharing**. The default option is **Turn on file and printer sharing**.

You can also configure HomeGroup connections here. This option allows you to configure how connections are made to other computers. You can choose **Allow Windows to manage HomeGroup connections** or **Use user accounts**

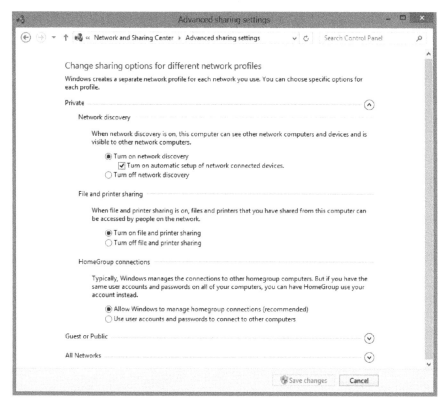

FIGURE 3.31 Private Network Profile

and passwords to connect to other computers. The default and recommended option is **Allow Windows to manage HomeGroup options**.

Guest or Public

The Guest or Public profile, as seen in Figure 3.32, includes settings for networks that are in public areas like coffee houses and airports. The first option is network discovery. Network discovery determines whether your computer can discover other devices on the network. It also determines whether or not your computer can be discovered by other computers. The first decision you must make is whether or not you want network discovery to be turned on. If it is turned on, then you must decide if you want to enable automatic setup of network connected devices.

The next option is file and printer sharing. File and printer sharing must be enabled for you to be able to share files and devices on your computer with other users on the network. You have two options here. You can either choose **Turn on file and printer sharing** or **Turn off file and printer sharing**.

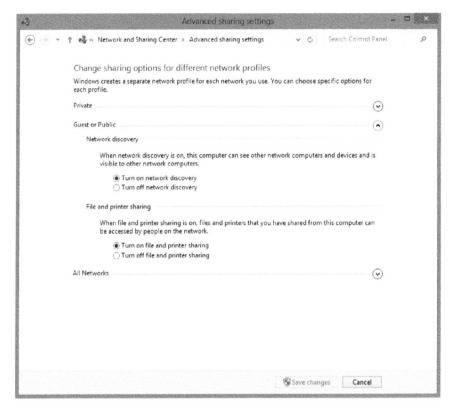

FIGURE 3.32 Guest or Public Network Profile

Domain

The Domain profile, as seen in Figure 3.33, includes settings that can be configured for systems that are a part of an Active Directory domain. The first option is network discovery. Network discovery determines whether your computer can discover other devices on the network. It also determines whether or not your computer can be discovered by other computers. The first decision you must make is whether or not you want network discovery to be turned on. If it is turned on, then you must decide if you want to enable automatic setup of network connected devices. The default option is **Turn off network discovery**.

The next option is file and printer sharing. File and printer sharing must be enabled for you to be able to share files and devices on your computer with other users on the network. You have two options here. You can either choose **Turn on file and printer sharing** or **Turn off file and printer sharing**. The default option is **Turn on file and printer sharing**.

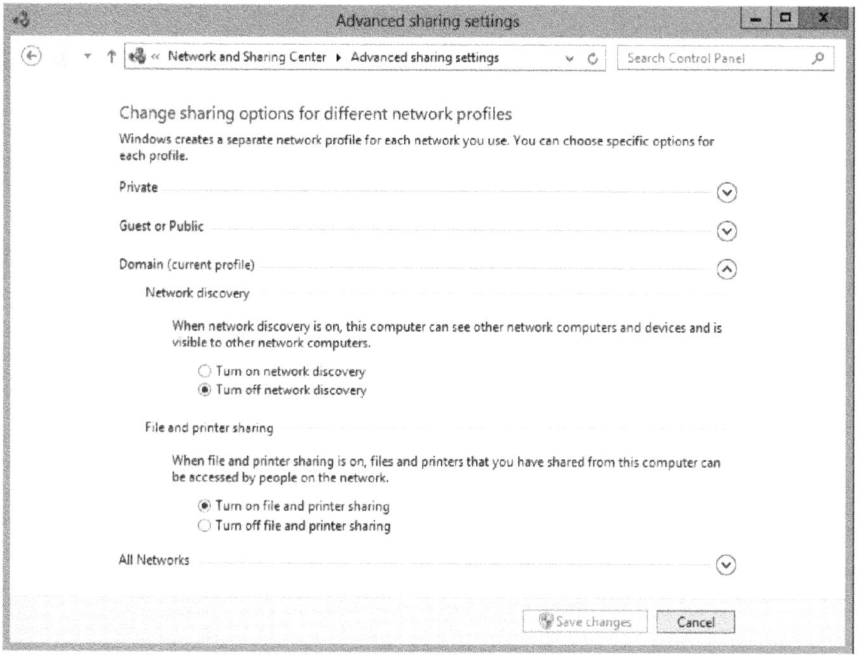

FIGURE 3.33 Advanced Sharing Settings Domain Profile

All Networks

The All Networks profile, as seen in Figure 3.34, includes settings for all network connections. The first option here is Public folder sharing. This option determines whether people on the network can access Public folders. There are two options available here: Turn on sharing so anyone with network access can read and write files in the Public folders and Turn off Public folder sharing. The default option is **Turn off Public folder sharing**.

Media streaming allows users to access pictures, videos, and other media files shared on the system. If you select the option for Choose media streaming options, it will bring up the Media streaming options window, as seen in Figure 3.35.

The option for File sharing connections allows you to configure encryption for file sharing connections. You have two options: **Use 128-bit encryption to help protect file sharing connections** and **Enable file sharing for devices that use 40- or 56-bit encryption**. Here, your choice is between security and compatibility. 128-bit security is more secure, but not all systems will be able to support 128-bit encryption. If you want to ensure compatibility with other systems you should use 40- or 56-bit encryption. The default option is **Use 128-bit encryption to help protect file sharing connections**.

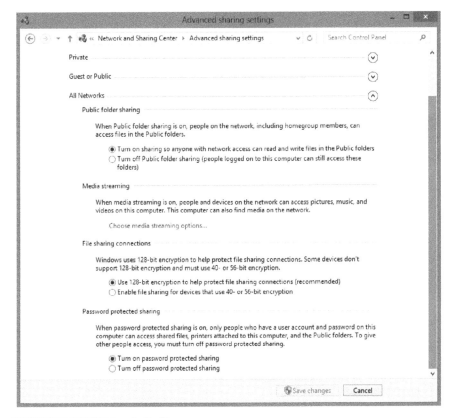

FIGURE 3.34 All Networks Profile

The last option is Password protected sharing. This option determines whether or not a user name and password are required to access shared files and printers. The two options available here are **Turn on password protected sharing** and **Turn off password protected sharing**. The default option is **Turn on password protected sharing**. This is the more secure option.

WINDOWS SERVER 2012 RESOURCE SHARING

File shares and other file services are provided by the File and Storage Services role. The base functionality for this role is installed on Windows Server 2012 systems by default. The role is configured using the File and Storage Services section of Server Manager, as seen in Figure 3.36.

New Shares are created using the New Share Wizard:

1. First, you are presented with the Select Profile screen, as seen in Figure 3.37. Here you much choose the type of share you want to create. After selecting the share profile, click Next.

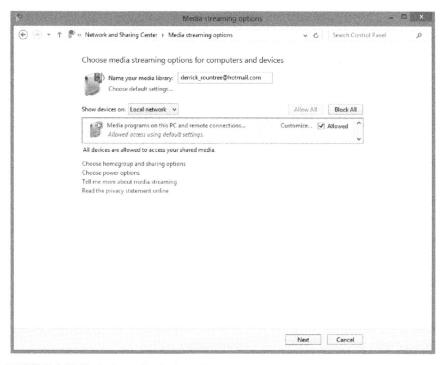

FIGURE 3.35 Media Streaming Options Window

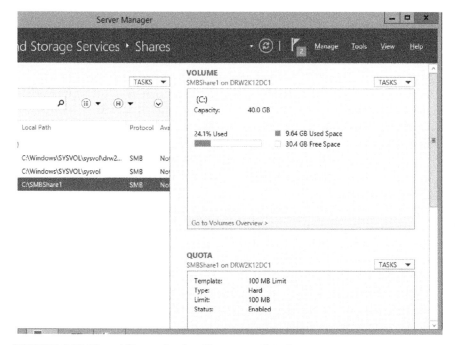

FIGURE 3.36 File and Storage Services Management Interface

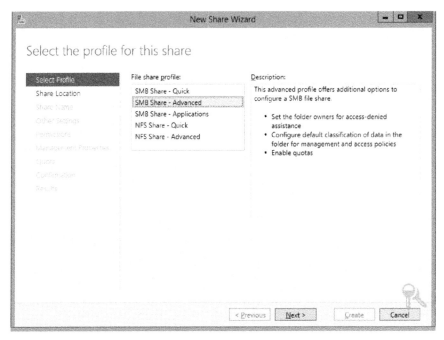

FIGURE 3.37 New Share Wizard Select Profile Screen

2. On the Share Location screen, as seen in Figure 3.38, you specify the volume or folder to be shared.

3. On the Share Name screen, as seen in Figure 3.39, you can specific a name for your share. You can also see the local path and the remote path to the share.

4. On the Other Settings screen, as seen in Figure 3.40, you can enable access-based enumeration, caching, and encrypted data access. These options can also be enabled by going to the properties of the share once it has been created. Enable the desired options, and click Next.

5. On the Permissions screen, as seen in Figure 3.41, you configure who will have what access to the share. Click Next.

6. On the Management Properties screen, as seen in Figure 3.42, you can choose folder usage properties. You can also specify an email address for the folder owner.

7. On the Quota screen, as seen in Figure 3.43, you can choose whether or not you want to implement a quota on the share. If you choose to implement a quota, you are asked to specify which template to use for the quota.

8. On the Confirmation screen, as seen in Figure 3.44, you verify the roles and services that are going to be installed on the system.

9. The Results screen, as seen in Figure 3.45, will give you information about the installation as it happens. You will then be notified when the installation is complete.

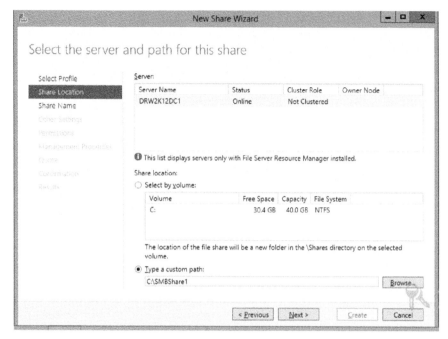

FIGURE 3.38 New Share Wizard Share Location Screen

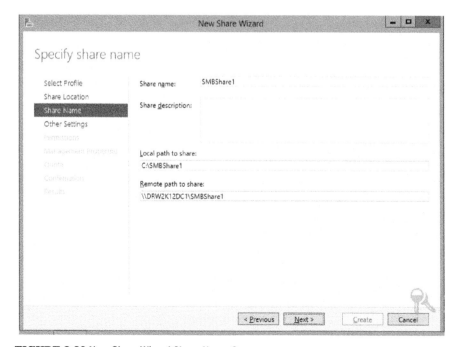

FIGURE 3.39 New Share Wizard Share Name Screen

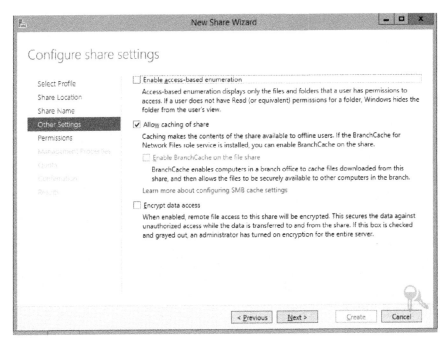

FIGURE 3.40 New Share Wizard Other Settings Screen

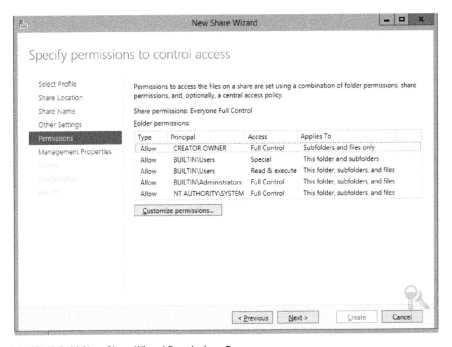

FIGURE 3.41 New Share Wizard Permissions Screen

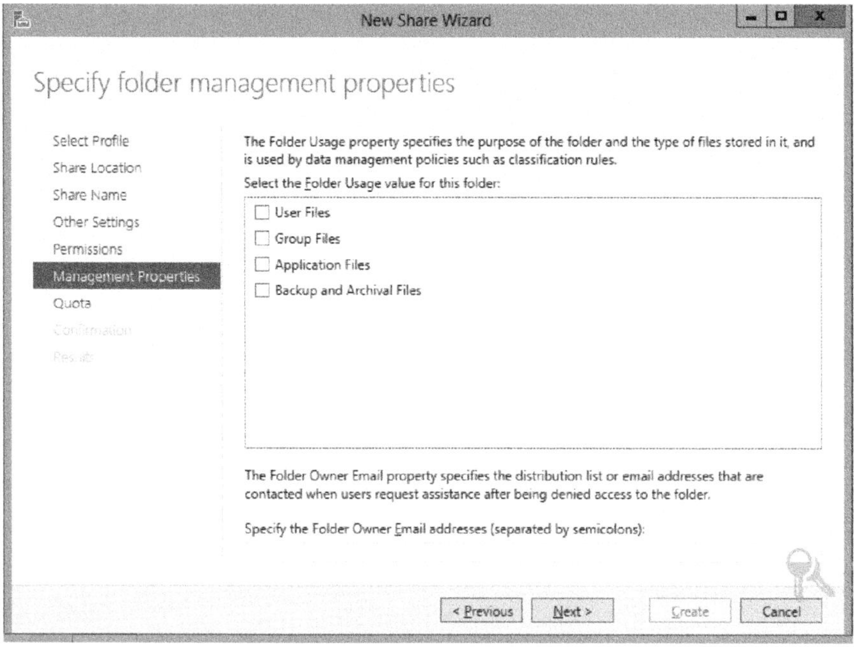

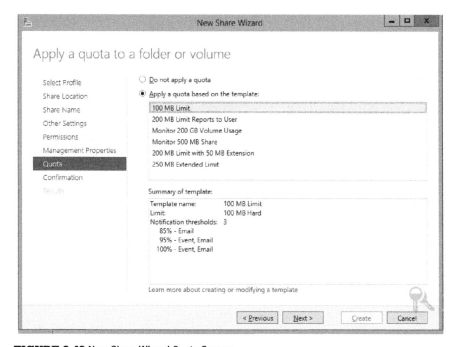

FIGURE 3.42 New Share Wizard Management Properties Screen

FIGURE 3.43 New Share Wizard Quota Screen

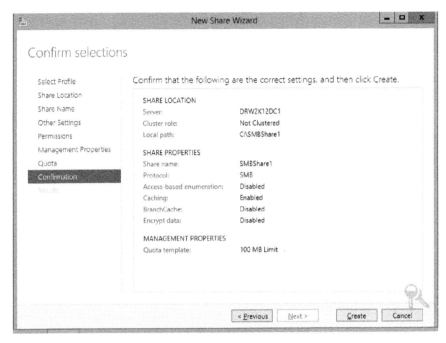

FIGURE 3.44 New Share Wizard Confirmation Screen

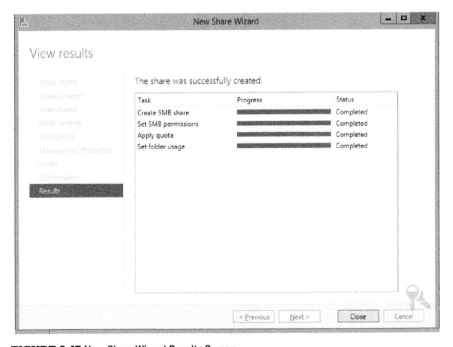

FIGURE 3.45 New Share Wizard Results Screen

Note: In order to use quotas, you have to install File Server Resource Manager. In the Add Roles and Features Wizard, it's located under File and Storage Services > File and iSCSI Services. In addition, you will be prompted to install the File Server Resource Manager Tool. It's located under Remote Administration Tools > Role Administration Tools > File Services Tools.

SUMMARY

Securing access to the network is a multistep process. You start with basic network connectivity and build upon that. Connections can be wired or wireless. Each type has its own vulnerabilities and security methods. You can use Windows Firewall to make sure these connections are secure. Windows Firewall allows you to specify which applications and connections you want to allow on the system. Windows Firewall with Advanced Security allows you to configure IPSec policies. IPSec provides a method for authenticating and encrypting connections.

Once you have secured your network connections, you then have to deal with securing basic services like resource sharing. Windows 8 and Windows Server 2012 have different methods for securing resource access. You can use HomeGroups, management groups, quotas, and other options.

Secure Remote Access

CONTENTS

INTRODUCTION

Remote system access can be used for management or to provide a remote environment for users.

Remote system access is a crucial part of any medium to large environment. It may not be feasible to always have physical access to your systems. In some cases, remote system access could be a convenience feature. In other cases it could be a necessity. Your systems may reside in a computer room or datacenter that is on another floor, or in another building. It could become quite an inconvenience to always have to walk over to the computer room or datacenter. Your systems could also reside in a datacenter in a remote location. This datacenter could be one owned by your company, or it could be space that you rent from someone else.

It's important that you set policies around what systems can be accessed remotely and how they can be accessed. Some methods or remote access are more secure than others. Some need to be specifically configured to provide a secure environment. Often times the default settings favor usability over security.

TELNET

Telnet has been used to connect to remote systems for a long time. It is still fairly widely used. Telnet consists of a server component and a client component. Windows 8 and Windows Server 2012 provide you with both of these components.

Telnet Server

The Telnet Server component allows a system to provide host services. Remote systems can connect to the host system and execute commands on the system. It can also be used for application services. Remote systems can use a Telnet connection to access applications on the host system.

Installing and Configuring the Telnet Server

The Telnet Server component is installed via Programs and Features. As seen in Figure 4.1, simply check the box for Telnet Server. This will install the Telnet Server service on your system.

Configuring the Telnet Service

There are several commands that let you configure the Telnet Server. The tlntadmn command allows you to configure your Telnet Server from a command prompt. As seen in Figure 4.2, the tlntadmn command has common options and command options. A few common commands are listed below.

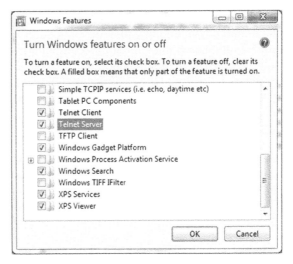

FIGURE 4.1 Windows Features Window

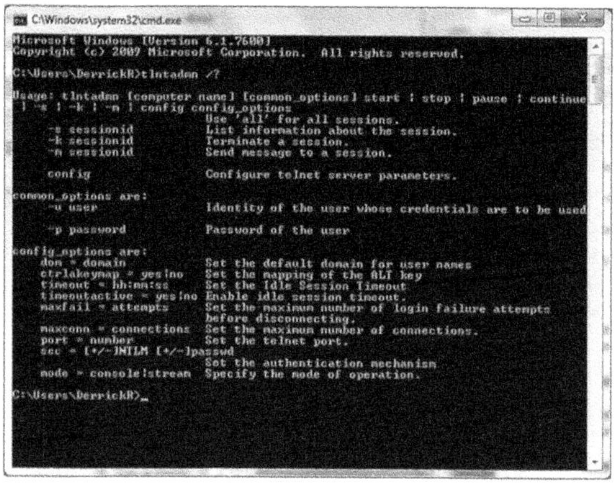

FIGURE 4.2 TIntadmn Command List

To start, stop, pause, or continue Telnet Server, the command syntax is:

> **tlntadmn [\\RemoteServer] [start] [stop] [pause] [continue]**
> **[-u UserName-p Password]**

To deactivate and disable NTLM authentication and switch to use only password authentication, the command is

> **tlntadmn config sec=-NTLM**

Further, to make Telnet session switch to streams mode for better display of Unix/Linux clients, enter:

> **tlntadmn config mode=stream**

Telnet Client

In order to make connections to a Telnet Server, you need a Telnet Client. Windows 8 and Windows 2012 include a basic Telnet Client for you to use. The Telnet Client is not enabled by default. It must be added. To install the Telnet Client you must install it using Programs and Features. As seen in Figure 4.3, you check the box for Telnet Client.

The Telnet Client is launched from a command prompt. The options available are as follows:

> -a: This option is used to automatically log on to the remote system. Telnet will attempt to use to currently logged on user to connect to the system.
> -e: This option allows you to enter an escape character that can be used to enter the Telnet Client prompt.

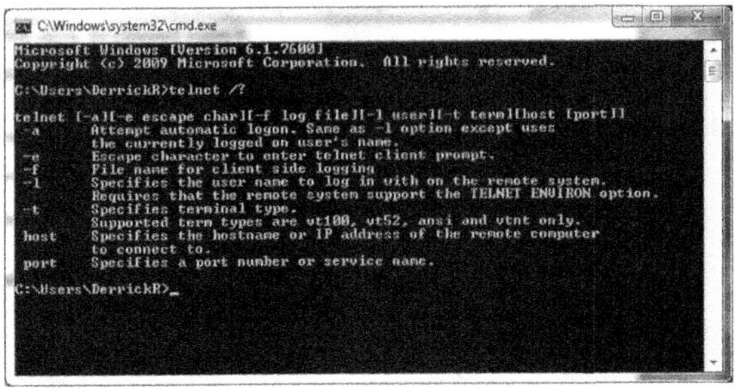

FIGURE 4.3 Telnet Command Help

-f: This option allows you to specify the name of a file that will be used for logging. The Telnet Client will log messages to this file.

-l: This option is used to specify user credentials that will used to log into the remote system.

Note: In order for this option to work, the remote system must support the TELNET ENVIRON option.

-t: This option allows you to specify the terminal type that will be used once the connection is made. You can choose from vt100, vt52, ansi, and vtnt.

-host: This option is where you specify the target computer. You can use an IP address or a hostname.

-port: This option allows you to specify a destination port.

Other Telnet Security Considerations

By default, Telnet connections are not encrypted. All the data is sent in plain text. If you use NTLM for authentication, then your credentials are protected, but the rest of the communication is still at risk. There are a few additional things you can do to secure your Telnet sessions. One of which is to encrypt your Telnet Traffic. Telnet communication can be encrypted using IPSec. This is done using Windows Firewall with Advanced Security.

REMOTE DESKTOP SERVICES

Remote Desktop Services has become the most common method for remotely accessing systems. Remote desktop functionality exists on server systems and client systems. Although, the functionality provided on each platform is slightly different. We will cover both scenarios.

Remote Desktop on Windows 8

Windows 8 systems provide some basic remote desktop functionality. You can use remote desktop to remotely run applications or to provide someone with help on their system.

FIGURE 4.4 Remote Tab of the System Properties Window

Remote Assistance

On the Remote tab of the System Properties window, you have the option to configure Remote Assistance. Remote Assistance allows someone on a remote computer to connect to your computer to provide you assistance. As seen in Figure 4.4, in the Remote Assistance section, check the option for Allow Remote Assistance connections to this computer.

Enabling Remote Assistance will cause Windows to open the appropriate tunnels in the Window Firewall to allow these connections.

Clicking the Advanced button, will bring up the Remote Assistance Settings window as shown in Figure 4.5. Here you can configure whether others can remotely control this system. If not, they can only view the console. You also have the option to configure a timeout for the Remote Assistance invitations that get sent. In addition, you configure it so that only computer running Windows Vista or later can connect to the system.

Remote Desktop

On the Remote tab of System Properties, you also have the ability to configure Remote Desktop. You can choose to either allow or prevent remote connections to the computer. If you allow connections, there are a few configuration

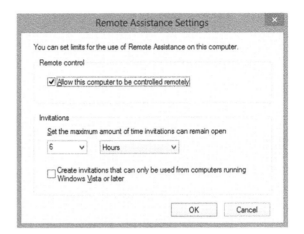

FIGURE 4.5 Remote Assistance Settings Window

options available to you. You have to Allow connections only from computer running Remote Desktop with Network Level Authentication. You also have option to specify which users are allowed to make Remote Desktop connections to the computer.

Note: By default members of the local Administrators group are allowed Remote Desktop access to the computer.

Remote Desktop Services Role on Windows Server 2012

In order to add Remote Desktop capabilities to your Windows Server 2012 system, you need to add the Remote Desktop Services Roles. You can use Remote Desktop Services to access virtual desktops, RemoteApp programs, and session-based desktops. Remote Desktop Service configuration and deployments can be very complex. You could write an entire book on just that. So, we'll go over a brief introduction of each, go through the installation, and focus on security-related configuration items:

1. One the Server Roles screen, select Remote Desktop Services. Click Next.
2. On the Features screen, click Next.
3. The Remote Desktop Services Information screen, as seen in Figure 4.6, will present you with information on Remote Desktop Services. Click Next.
4. You will then be presented with the Role Services screen, as seen in Figure 4.7. You can choose the following: Remote Desktop Session Host, Remote Desktop Virtualization Host, Remote Desktop Gateway, Remote Desktop Web Access, Remote Desktop Connection Broker, or Remote Desktop Licensing.

FIGURE 4.6 Remote Desktop Services Information Screen

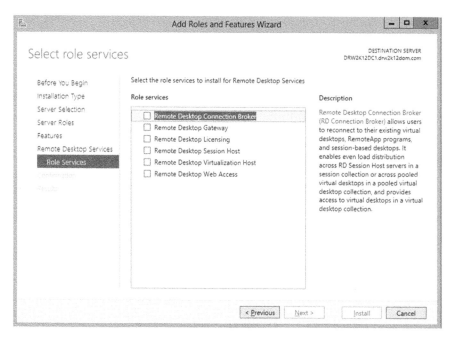

FIGURE 4.7 Remote Desktop Services Role Services

Since it would not be recommended to install all of these role services on the same system, we will cover each role service individually. We won't be covering the Remote Desktop Virtualization Host or Remote Desktop Licensing.

Note: After you have installed the Remote Desktop Services Roles, the role services will appear on the Server Roles screen, and not on the Role Services screen.

Remote Desktop Session Host Role Service

The Remote Desktop Session Host is the service that is comparable to the traditional Terminal Services role. Remote Desktop Session Host allows you to deliver session-based desktops and RemoteApp programs. Users connect to a Remote Desktop or RemoteApp session on the server and the applications will integrate directly with their client environment.

Installation and Initial Configuration

1. On the Role Features screen, select Session Host.
2. You will then see a window, as seen in Figure 4.8, notifying you of required features that must be installed with the Session Host role feature. Click Add features.
3. The Session Host Confirmation screen, as seen in Figure 4.9, will display what will be installed with the Session Host role feature.
4. The Results screen will let you know the progress of your installation and whether the install completed successfully.

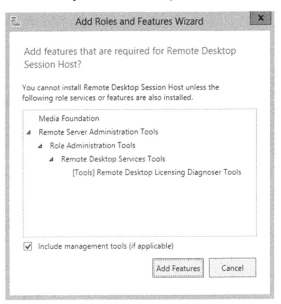

FIGURE 4.8 Session Host Required Features

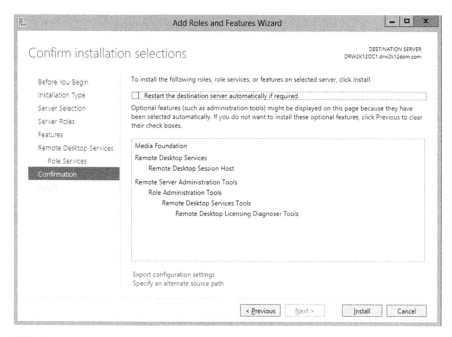

FIGURE 4.9 Session Host Confirmation Screen

Remote Desktop Gateway Role Service

The Remote Desktop Gateway service is used to provide secure remote access to the features delivered by the other Remote Desktop Services. You can use Remote Desktop Gateway to connect to session-based desktops, RemoteApp programs, and virtual desktops. Using Remote Desktop Gateway, you can be at a location external to your corporate network and still connect to servers and resources located internally to the network.

Installation and Initial Configuration

1. On the Role Features screen, select Remote Desktop Gateway.
2. You will then see a window, as seen in Figure 4.10, notifying you of required features that must be installed with the Remote Desktop Gateway role feature. Click Add features.
3. On the Features Screen. Click Next.
4. The Remote Desktop Gateway Confirmation screen, as seen in Figure 4.11, will display what will be installed with the Remote Desktop Gateway role feature.
5. The Results screen will let you know the progress of your installation and whether the install completed successfully.

FIGURE 4.10 Remote Desktop Gateway Required Features

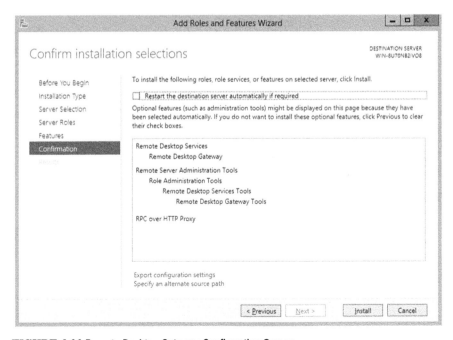

FIGURE 4.11 Remote Desktop Gateway Confirmation Screen

Remote Desktop Web Access Role Service

Remote Desktop Web Access makes it easy for you to access RemoteApp sessions and remote session desktop. You can access them either via the Start Menu or via a web browser. You can see your published resources in either a session collection or a virtual desktop collection.

Installation and Initial Configuration

1. On the Role Services screen, select Remote Desktop Web Access. Click Next.
2. On the Features screen, click Next.
3. The Remote Desktop Web Access Confirmation screen, as seen in Figure 4.12.
4. The Results screen will let you know the progress of your installation and whether the install completed successfully.

Remote Desktop Connection Client

The Remote Desktop Client is used to connect to a system running Remote Desktop Services. Like the Remote Desktop Role, there are many options available with the Remote Desktop Client. So, again, we will give a basic overview of the client and focus on the security-related features.

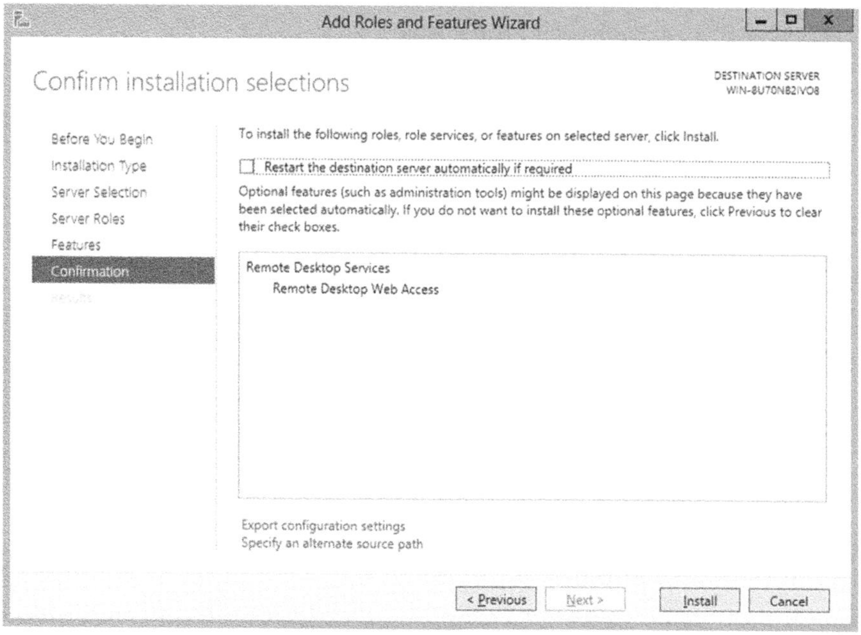

FIGURE 4.12 Remote Desktop Web Access Confirmation Screen

You can start the Remote Desktop Client using a command line or by starting the GUI directly. To start the Remote Desktop Connection Client from a command line, you use the mstsc command. The following options are available with the command:

Connection file: This option allows you to specify a .rdp file to make a connection. .rdp files represent saved settings.

V:server:port: This option is used to specify the remote system you want to connect to. You can use a hostname or an IP address.

/admin: This option is used to make a connection to the console of the remote system. Certain functions and application installations can only be performed in admin mode.

/f: This option started the Remote Desktop session in full screen mode.

/w: This option can be used to specify the width for the remote desktop window.

/h: This option can be used to specify the height for the remote desktop window.

/public: This option runs remote desktop in public mode. In public mode, passwords and images will not be cached. Public mode is recommended for use on public computers.

/span: This option is used to create a Remote Desktop session with the same height and width as the local virtual session. This may require spanning across multiple monitors. In order for this to work, the local monitors have to be configured in a rectangle.

/multimon: This option is used to make the Remote Desktop session the same as the current client monitor settings.

/edit: This option is used to edit a .rdp file.

/migrate: This option is used to migrate legacy connection files to the newer .rdp format.

FIGURE 4.13 Remote Desktop Client

By default, the Remote Desktop Client will look like Figure 4.13 when launched. You can see the computer you will be connecting to and the user credentials that will be used. If you want to see more connection properties, you need to select Show options. This will bring up the various property tabs. These include: General, Display, Local Resources, Programs, Experience, and Advanced.

General

As seen in Figure 4.14, the General tab of the Remote Desktop Connection Client is where you specify basic connection information.

Logon Settings

Computer: This is where you specify the remote computer to which you would like to connect. You can use a NetBIOS name, an FQDN, or an IP address.

Username: This is where you can specify the username you want to use to make the connection.

Allow me to save credentials.

Connection Settings

This section is used to work with connection files, or .rdp files. You can open an existing connection, or save your current to a connection file.

FIGURE 4.14 General Tab of the Remote Desktop Connection Client

Display

The Display tab is where you will set the display settings for your Remote Desktop session. You can configure screen size and color depth. You can also configure whether or not to show the connection bar.

Display Configuration

Display Configuration allows you to configure the screen size. The options are as follows:

- 640 × 480,
- 800 × 600,
- 1024 × 768,
- 1280 × 800,
- 1280 × 720,
- 1280 × 768,
- Full screen.

Colors

Colors allow you to configure the color depth. The options are as follows:

- High color (15 bit).
- High color (16 bit).
- True color (24 bit).
- Highest color (32 bit).

The final option in this page is Display the connection bar when I use fill screen. Click the box if you want the connection bar shown.

Local Resources

The Local Resources tab is an important one. It is used to configure whether or not resources on the client system can be accessed inside the Remote Desktop session. The configuration includes Remote audio, Keyboard, and Local devices and resources. From a security standpoint the Local devices and resources option is the most important.

Remote Audio

The Remote audio option is used to configure audio playback and recording. The options are as follows:

- Remote audio playback:
  - Play on this computer.
  - Do not play.
  - Play on remote computer.

- Remote audio recording:
  - Record from this computer.
  - Do not record.

Keyboard

The keyboard option allows you to configure what happens when key combinations are pressed. The options are as follows:
Apply Windows key combinations:

  - On this computer.
  - On the remote computer.
  - Only when using the full screen.

Local Devices and Resources

You have to be careful when allowing local resources to be used within a Remote Desktop session. If you enable local resource usage, then the server you are connecting to will have access to resources on your system. If you do not trust the remote system, you should not enable local resource usage. You can configure the following items:

- Printers.
- Clipboard.
- Smart cards.
- Ports.
- Drives.
- Drives that I plug in later.
- Other supported Plug and Play (PnP) devices.
- Devices that I plug in later.

One of the key items that can be configured here are disk drives. Enabling disk drives can potentially give harmful code on a remote server access to all the files on your local system. So, you need to be especially careful when enabling this option.

Programs

The Programs tab allows you to specify a program that will start when the connection is made. This is a program that will run on the remote system. This can be a very useful feature. But, it can also be dangerous. A .rdp file could be configured that would run a malicious file when a connection is made. If you are running a Remote Desktop connection that has specified a program to run on connection, you need to ensure that the program is not malicious.

Start a Program

The options in the Start a program section are as follows.

Start the following program on connection:

- Program path and file name.
- Start in the following folder.

Experience

The Experience tab allows you to configure options that affect the user experience.

Performance

The Performance section allows you to configure options based on your connection speed. These different options use up different amounts of bandwidth. So, based on your connection, the Remote Desktop Connection Client will list a recommended configuration that is optimized for your bandwidth.

The **Choose your connection speed to optimize performance** option allows you to select the bandwidth for your connection. The options are as follows:

- Modem 56 Kbps.
- Low-speed broadband (256 Kbps–2 Mbps).
- Satellite (2–16 Mbps with high latency).
- High-speed broadband (2–10 Mbps).
- LAN (10 Mbps or higher with high latency).
- WAN (10 Mbps or higher).

Based on the bandwidth option chosen, the following features will be enabled or disabled by default:

- Desktop background.
- Font smoothing.
- Desktop composition.
- Show window contents while dragging.
- Menu and window animation.
- Visual styles.

The Experience tab also allows you to enable the **Persistent bitmap caching** and **Reconnect if the connection is dropped** options.

Advanced

Finally, we have the Advanced tab. There are two advanced options available: Server authentication and Connect from anywhere. Both of these options are security related.

Server Authentication

Server authentication is used to verify that the server you are connecting to is the server you intended to connect to. The strength of the authentication is configured using the Local Security Policy on your client system.

What you configure here is what should be done if the server authentication fails. The options are as follows:

- *Connect and don't warn me:* This is the least secure option. If the server authentication fails, the connection will still be made. In addition, the user will not be notified of the failure.
- *Warn me:* This option is more secure and it gives the user a choice. If the server authentication fails, the user will be notified. The user can then choose whether or not to make the connection.
- *Do not connect:* This is the most secure option. If the server authentication fails, the connection will not be made to the remote server.

Connect from Anywhere

This section allows you to configure settings for using a Remote Desktop Gateway. An RD Gateway allows you to secure Remote Desktop connections from outside of your organization. The options are as follows:

- Connection Settings:
    - Automatically detect RD Gateway server settings.
    - Use these RD Gateway server settings:
        - Server name.
        - Logon method:
            - Allow me to select later.
            - Ask for password (NTLM).
            - Smart card.
        - Bypass RD Gateway server for local address.
    - Do not use an RD Gateway Server.
- Logon Settings:
    - Use my RD Gateway credentials for the remote computer.

Connection Files

Connection files are used to save a specific set of setting for a Remote Desktop connection. This keeps you from having to repeatedly set the same settings for a specific connection. It also allows you to share connection settings with other users.

Creating a .rdp file:

1. Launch the Remote Desktop Client.
2. Configure the client with the options you want.
3. Choose Show Options.
4. On the General Tab, click Save or Save As. Save will save to current connection file if one was already specified. Save As will allow you to specify a connection or create a new one.

Modifying a .rdp file.

There are two methods that can be used to modify a .rdp file. The first is by using notepad. Figure 4.15 shows a .rdp opened in notepad.

```
screen mode id:i:2
use multimon:i:0
desktopwidth:i:1400
desktopheight:i:1050
session bpp:i:32
winposstr:s:0,3,0,0,800,600
compression:i:1
keyboardhook:i:2
audiocapturemode:i:0
videoplaybackmode:i:1
connection type:i:7
networkautodetect:i:1
bandwidthautodetect:i:1
displayconnectionbar:i:1
enableworkspacereconnect:i:0
disable wallpaper:i:1
allow font smoothing:i:0
allow desktop composition:i:0
disable full window drag:i:1
disable menu anims:i:1
disable themes:i:0
disable cursor setting:i:0
bitmapcachepersistenable:i:1
full address:s:drw2k12s1
audiomode:i:0
redirectprinters:i:1
redirectcomports:i:0
redirectsmartcards:i:1
redirectclipboard:i:1
redirectposdevices:i:0
autoreconnection enabled:i:1
authentication level:i:2
prompt for credentials:i:0
negotiate security layer:i:1
remoteapplicationmode:i:0
alternate shell:s:
shell working directory:s:
gatewayhostname:s:gateway.server.com
gatewayusagemethod:i:2
gatewaycredentialssource:i:0
gatewayprofileusagemethod:i:1
promptcredentialonce:i:1
use redirection server name:i:0
rdgiskdcproxy:i:0
kdcproxyname:s:
drivestoredirect:s:C:\;
```

FIGURE 4.15 Text from a .rdp File

The other option is to use the Remote Desktop Client with the edit option:

1. Launch the Remote Desktop using mstsc /edit <filename>.
2. Make the desired changes.
3. On the General Tab, click Save.

REMOTE ACCESS ROLE

The Remote Access role has two components: DirectAccess and RRAS VPN and RRAS Routing. In this book, we will only be covering DirectAccess. DirectAccess allows remote connectivity to your corporate network without the need for a VPN. DirectAccess uses IPSec to create a secure connection between the client system and the corporate network.

Remote Access Role Installation and Configuration

1. On the Server Roles screen, as seen in Figure 4.16, select Remote Access.
2. When you select the Remote Access role, a window, as seen in Figure 4.17, will pop up notifying you of features that must be installed with the Remote Access role. Click Add Features. Click Next.
3. The Remote Access role Overview screen, as seen in Figure 4.18, will provide you an overview of the Remote Access role.

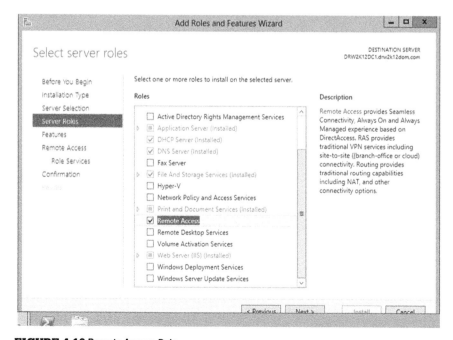

FIGURE 4.16 Remote Access Role

FIGURE 4.17 Remote Access Role Required Features

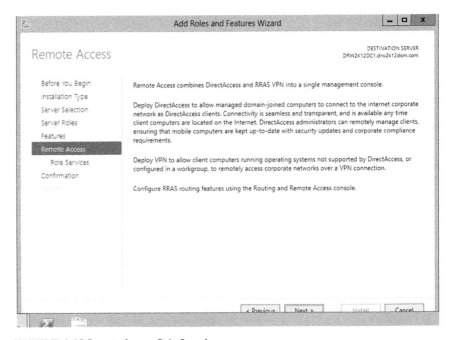

FIGURE 4.18 Remote Access Role Overview

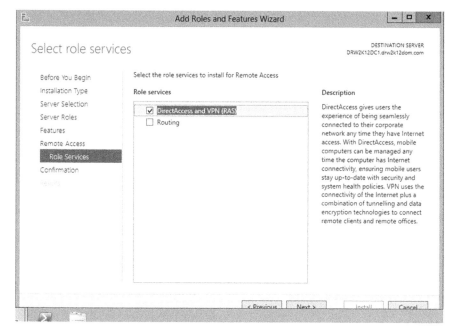

FIGURE 4.19 Remote Access Role Services

4. On the Remote Access Role Services screen, as seen in Figure 4.19, you
   have the option to install DirectAccess and VPN (RAS) and Routing. Select
   DirectAccess and VPN (RAS). Click Next.
5. The Remote Access role Confirmation screen, as seen in Figure 4.20, will
   display the features and services that will be installed with Remote Access.
6. The Results screen will let you know the progress of your installation and
   whether the install completed successfully.

After the Remote Access role is installed, it must be configured:

1. From Server Manager Notifications area, you can launch the Configure
   Remote Access Getting Started Wizard, as seen in Figure 4.21.
2. Select Deploy both DirectAccess and VPN. The system will check to see if
   the prerequisites have been met. Then the configuration begins.
3. On the Remote Access Server Setup screen, as seen in Figure 4.22, select
   the appropriate network topology. For this example, we will be selecting
   Behind an edge device (*with a single network adapter*). You also need to enter
   the public IP address that will be used to access the Remote Access server.
   Click Next.
4. The last screen of the wizard, as seen in Figure 4.23, allows you to edit the
   settings you have configured. Click Finish to have your settings applied.

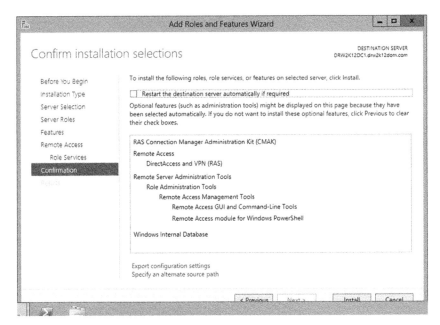

FIGURE 4.20 Remote Access Confirmation Screen

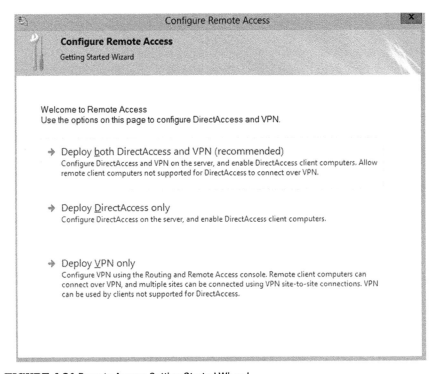

FIGURE 4.21 Remote Access Getting Started Wizard

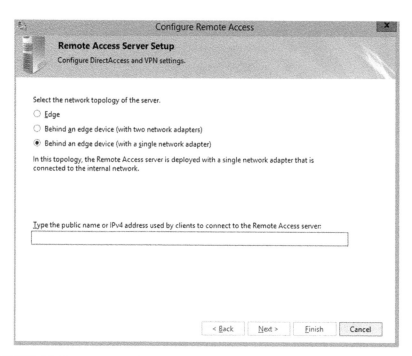

FIGURE 4.22 Remote Access Server Setup Screen

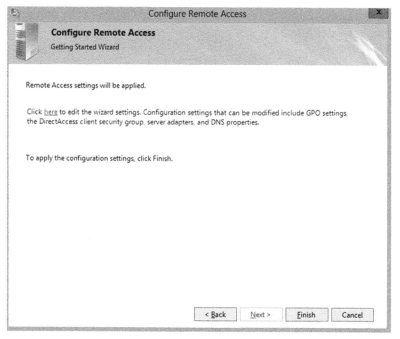

FIGURE 4.23 Remote Access Apply Settings Screen

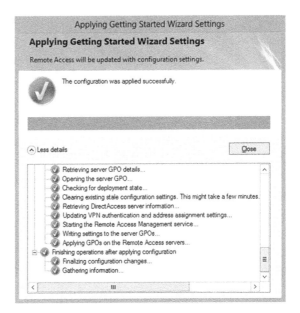

FIGURE 4.24 Remote Access Applying Settings Window

5. The Applying Settings window, as seen in Figure 4.24, will appear letting you the know status of your configuration and whether your settings were applied successfully.

DirectAccess

DirectAccess is managed in the Remote Access Management Console. The Configuration node, as seen in Figure 4.25, allows you to edit the configuration of your DirectAccess instance. You can configure settings for your remote clients, remote access server, infrastructure servers, and application servers. The Dashboard node allows you to view information on your DirectAccess service and your VPN service. The Operations Status node will provide you the status information for DirectAccess and VPN. The Remote Client Status node will show you the status of clients currently connected to the system. The Reporting Node can be used to generate reports on service activity.

Note: Inbox Accounting must be configured to use the Reporting Node.

VPN

Remote Access VPN Settings are configured in the Routing and Remote Access Console, as seen in Figure 4.26. You can configure packet filtering to protect your network against malicious traffic. You can configure your VPN to only

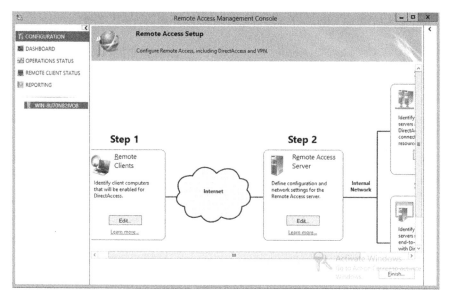

FIGURE 4.25 Remote Access Management Console Configuration Node

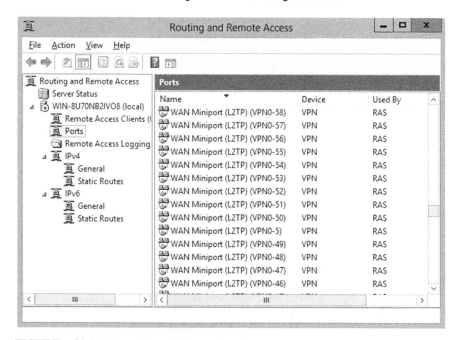

FIGURE 4.26 Routing and Remote Access Console

allow access to specific services and ports. You can turn on logging, so that you can monitor usage. You can configure secure authentication methods and the use of PKI.

NETWORK POLICY AND ACCESS SERVICES

Network Policy and Access Services (NPAS) is used to provide secure remote access. This access is provided via a few different methods. NPAS is used to deploy RADIUS, Network Access Protection (NAP), and secure access points. NPAS consists of three role services: Network Policy Server (NPS), Health Registration Authority (HRA), and Host Credential Authorization Policy (HCAP).

NPS functions as a central management server for protecting network access. NPS is a key component for configuring NAP in your environment. It also allows you to provide secure wired and wireless access via RADIUS and PEAP.

HRA is a NAP component used with IPSec enforcement. HRA will issue a certificate to clients that pass the health check.

HCAP allows you to integrate your Microsoft NAP solution with a Cisco Network Access Control Server. This allows you to perform evaluations and authorizations for Cisco 802.1X access clients.

NPAS Installation and Configuration

1. On the Server Roles screen, as seen in Figure 4.27, select Network Policy and Access Services role.
2. When you select the Network Policy and Access Services role, you will be present with a set of required features that must also be installed, as seen in Figure 4.28. Click Add Features.
3. On the Feature screen, click Next.
4. The Network Policy and Access Services Information screen, as seen in Figure 4.29, will give you information about Network Policy and Access Services role. Click Next.
5. The Role Services screen, as seen in Figure 4.30, allows you to specify which services you want the role to perform. There are three options: Network Policy Server, Health Registration Authority, and Host Credential Authorization Protocol.
6. If you choose to install the Health Registration Authority role service, then you will also be presented with a screen, as seen in Figure 4.31, that will display additional features that must be installed. Click Add Features.
7. On the Certification Authority screen, as seen in Figure 4.32, you must select a CA to be used for issuing certificates. Click Next.
8. On the Authentication Requirements screen, as seen in Figure 4.33, you select the type of authentication that must be used when requesting health certificates. Requiring domain authentication is the more secure option.

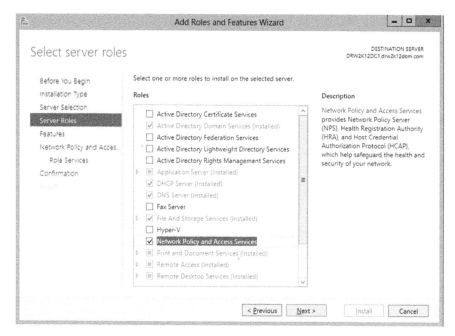

FIGURE 4.27 Server Roles Screen

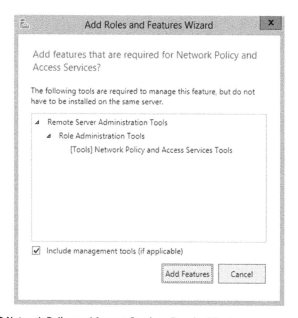

FIGURE 4.28 Network Policy and Access Services Required Features

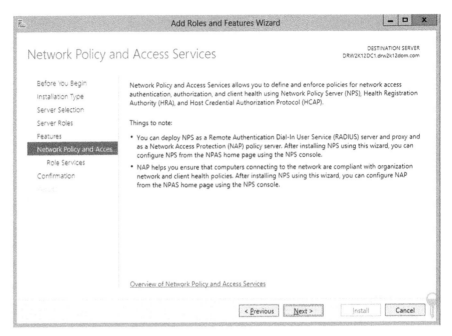

FIGURE 4.29 Network Policy and Access Services Information Screen

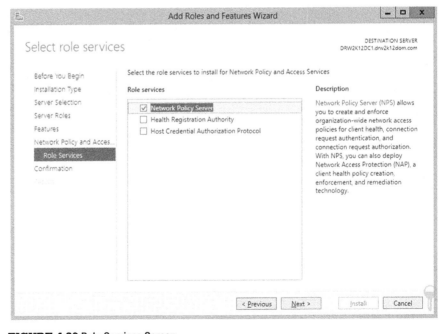

FIGURE 4.30 Role Services Screen

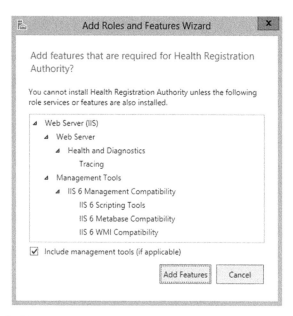

FIGURE 4.31 Health Registration Authority Required Features

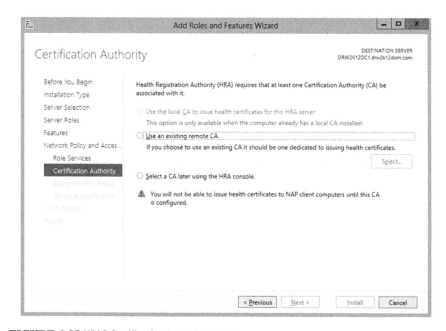

FIGURE 4.32 NPAS Certification Authority Screen

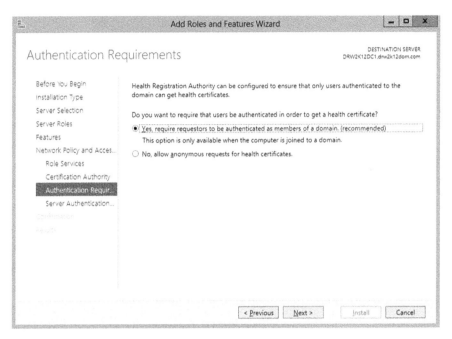

FIGURE 4.33 NPAS Authentication Requirements Screen

But, if your system is not part of a domain you will only be able to allow anonymous requests. Click Next.

9. On the Server Authentication screen, as seen in Figure 4.34, you can choose an SSL certificate to use for encrypting network traffic. Enabling SSL is the more secure option. If you don't have a certificate currently configured on the system, then you can choose to specify one later. Click Next.

10. The Confirmation screen, as seen in Figure 4.35, will show you which roles and services will be installed. Click Install.

11. The Results screen will let you know the progress of the installation and whether NPAS was installed successfully or not. The Results screen will also let you know that a restart is required to complete the installation.

Network Policy Server

As seen in Figure 4.36, NPS includes a configuration wizard that allows you to do a basic configuration. You have three options: Network Access Protection (NAP), RADIUS server for Dial-up or VPN Connections, and RADIUS server for 802.1X Wireless or Wired Connections.

FIGURE 4.34 NPAS Server Authentication Screen

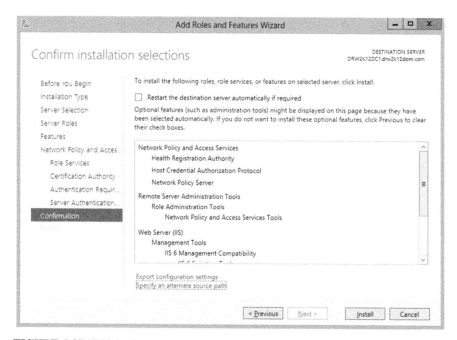

FIGURE 4.35 NPAS Confirmation Screen

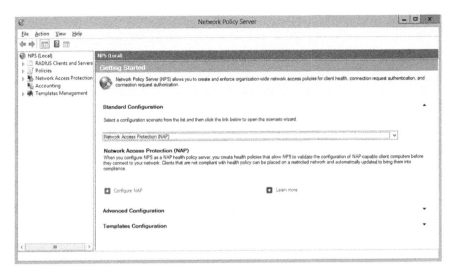

FIGURE 4.36 NPS Configuration

Health Registration Authority

In the Health Registration Authority console, as seen in Figure 4.37, you can configure your certification authority settings and your request policies. Your request policies consist of two different policies: cryptographic policies and transport policies.

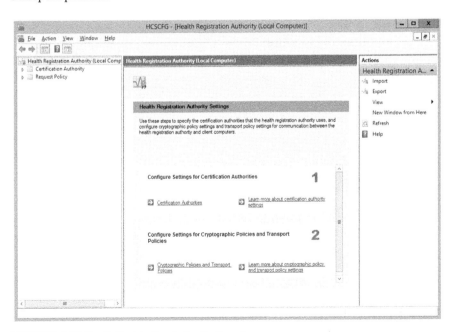

FIGURE 4.37 Health Registration Authority Console

Host Credential Authorization Protocol

Host Credential Authorization Protocol is configured using the Connection Request Policy node of the Network Policy Server console. When creating the new policy, you would choose HCAP Server for the network access server type.

SUMMARY

Secure remote access can be provided in many different ways. You can use Telnet for basic console access. Remote Desktop provides a much richer desktop experience. The Remote Access role provides remote network access, so you can access multiple devices on a network, not just a single device.

CHAPTER 5

Internet Connection Security

- Internet Explorer Security
- Internet Options

CONTENTS

Although the threat from internal attacks is dangerous, the most dangerous risk is still from external threats. Most external threats are done through the Internet. It's important to secure your systems from these Internet threats. These can present themselves in many different forms. You need to make sure you understand these different forms and are ready to combat the threats.

Internet security starts with the web browser. The web browser represents most client systems' main entry point to the Internet. The web browser also represents the most attacked application on a client system. Attackers don't just attack the web browser itself; they use it as a gateway to deliver other system attacks. Most users do not know how to properly secure their web browsers to help protect themselves from attacks.

The web browser is not the only application used to make Internet- or web-based connections. These other methods have to be secured also. Windows provides the Internet Options applet for securing these connections.

In this chapter, we will only be covering how to make secure Internet connections. We will not be covering how to provide secure applications and Internet-based services. So we will not go over IIS (Internet Information Server) or Application Server security in this chapter.

INTERNET EXPLORER SECURITY

Windows systems now come with two versions of Internet Explorer: the classic version and the new Windows Store app version. For the purposes of this chapter, when we talk about Internet Explorer, we are talking about the

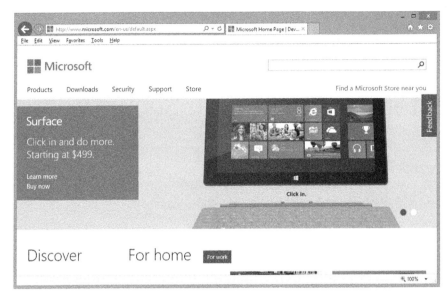

FIGURE 5.1 Internet Explorer Domain Highlighting

classic version, unless otherwise noted. By default, Internet Explorer does put some measure in place to protect the user's system. But, there are many more options that could be enabled to make the browser more secure, if you know what you're doing. This is what we are going to go over. We'll cover the different options available with Internet Explorer, what they mean, and how they are configured. Some option will only be covered briefly in this section because they will be covered more in depth in the Internet Options section.

Domain Highlighting

Windows uses a feature called domain highlighting to denote the top-level domain that is being accessed inside Internet Explorer. As seen in Figure 5.1, when domain highlighting is enabled, Internet Explorer will highlight the top-level domain in black; the rest of the URL will be gray. This purpose of this visual indicator is to make users more aware of the domain they are connecting to. The intent is to help prevent phishing attacks and other attacks where the user is redirected to a site they did not intend to visit.

Frequently Visited Sites

Internet Explorer will show you a listing of sites that you frequently visit, as seen in Figure 5.2. This allows you to easily choose a site that you want to revisit. The problem is that displaying this information allows anyone to easily

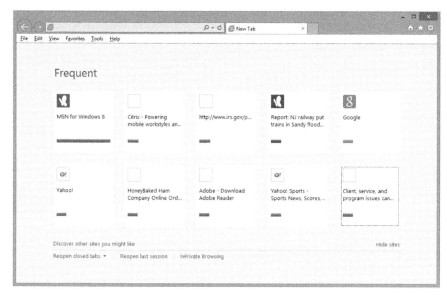

FIGURE 5.2 Internet Explorer Frequently Used Sites

see what sites you frequently visit, simply by looking over your shoulder. This would make it easier for an attacker to figure out what site they may use in a phishing attack against you.

If you are concerned about this risk, Internet Explorer allows you to mitigate the risk by hiding the list. This can be done by simply clicking Hide sites. The site list will then be hidden as seen in Figure 5.3.

Safety Features
There are a set of features included with Internet Explorer, that could be considered safety features. In fact, if you click the shortcut Tools menu on the top right of the Internet Explorer windows, as seen in Figure 5.4, there is a subcategory called Safety where these features reside. The features listed here are Delete Browsing History, InPrivate Browsing, Tracking Protection, ActiveX Filtering, Webpage privacy policy, Check this website, Turn off SmartScreen filter, and Report unsafe website.

Note: Most of the features listed under the Safety heading are also available from the Tools dropdown menu, but Webpage privacy policy is not.

Delete Browsing History
Browsing history is a list of recently visited web sites. The concern here is more about privacy than general security. If you do not delete your browsing

FIGURE 5.3 Internet Explorer Hidden Site List

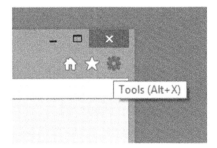

FIGURE 5.4 Shortcut Tools Menu

history, then anyone with access to system may be able to see what sites you visited. You may not want others to have access to this information, especially if one of the sites visited was related to some health issue you may be experiencing. In addition, having access to your browsing history may give an attacker additional info they could use to initiate a phishing or social engineering attack. If they know what sites you visit, that could give them an idea of a site to impersonate to try to get you to enter your personal information.

Choosing this option will bring up the Delete Browsing History window. This is the same window seen when selecting Delete from the Browsing History section on the General tab of Internet Options, so we will cover these options more in depth in the Internet Options section of the chapter.

InPrivate Browsing

InPrivate Browsing is designed to keep web sessions private. This is twofold. First, it's supposed to keep other users from being able to tell what websites you visited within your browsing sessions. Second, it's supposed to keep websites from being able to tell that you visited them before.

Selecting this option will open an InPrivate Browsing session. A new Internet Explorer window will open showing the message seen in Figure 5.5. While using InPrivate Browsing, Internet Explorer will not store information about your session.

Note: You have to be careful when using InPrivate Browsing. It may not be as private as you think. There may be certain add-ons configured in your browser that may be gathering and storing information. So, if you want truly private browsing, you need to verify the add-ons that you currently have enabled.

Tracking Protection

Tracking Protection allows you to control which websites can track information from your system. You can prevent websites from tracking information directly or indirectly. Many times you will visit one website, but that website will send your information to another website. Tracking Protection allows you

FIGURE 5.5 InPrivate Browsing Indicator

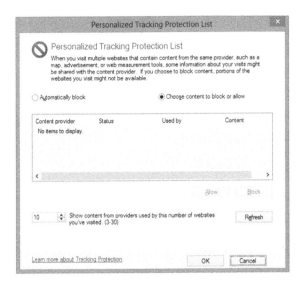

FIGURE 5.6 Personalized Tracking Protection List Window

to prevent this. With Tracking Protection, you can specify what sites can receive your information.

Selecting this option will bring up the Manage Add-ons windows. Here, there is an Add-on Type called Tracking Protection. You can download an already created list or you can configure your own Personalized Tracking Protection List, as seen in Figure 5.6.

ActiveX Filtering

ActiveX controls are Internet Explorer plug-ins that can be used to greatly enhance the user experience on various websites. ActiveX controls can also cause problems. In some cases they can lead to browser instability.

Selecting this option will enable ActiveX Filtering. You can know when ActiveX Filtering is enabled because there will be a check mark next to the option. With ActiveX Filtering enabled, you can browse websites without ActiveX controls being enabled. You can disable ActiveX controls in Internet Options, but this is an easier temporary solution. You can use it to test whether or not ActiveX controls are causing issues that you are having with your browser.

Webpage Privacy Policy

Many webpages have privacy policies. This policy explains what the website is doing to protect your privacy. The policy may also detail any information that is being collected by the website.

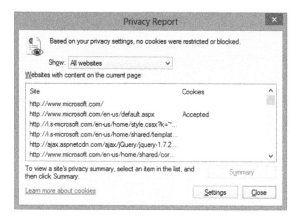

Figure 5.7 Privacy Report Window

Selecting this option will bring up the Privacy Report window, as seen in Figure 5.7.

If you select a site and click Summary, it will open the Privacy Policy window as shown in Figure 5.8. This window will display the privacy policy for the site, if one exists. You can select how cookies should be handled for the site. Selecting Settings will bring up the Privacy tab of the Internet Options applet, which will be covered later.

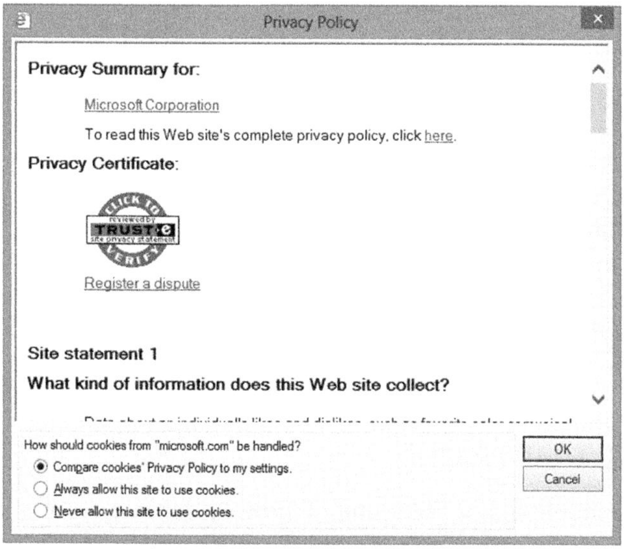

FIGURE 5.8 Privacy Policy Window

FIGURE 5.9 SmartScreen Filter Warning Message

Check This Website

The feature Check this website will send information about the current website to Microsoft where it can be analyzed to determine if the site is malicious. Choosing this option will bring up the SmartScreen Filter warning message seen in Figure 5.9. This ensures that you are intended to send information from your system to Microsoft.

Turn Off SmartScreen Filter

SmartScreen Filter is actually a collection of smaller features. It helps protect you from malicious websites and file downloads. SmartScreen Filter will check websites you visit to determine if they are malicious or not. SmartScreen Filter will check the website against a list of known malicious sites. It will also examine the webpage itself to determine if it exhibits characteristics known for malicious sites. SmartScreen Filter protects you from malicious files, by checking the files you download against a list of known malicious files.

Selecting this option will bring up the SmartScreen Filter window as seen in Figure 5.10. Here you have the option to turn SmartScreen Filter on or off depending on if it is currently enabled or not.

Report Unsafe Website

Selecting this option will bring up a webpage, as seen in Figure 5.11, that can be used to report the current website to Microsoft. This will help Microsoft to build a list of potentially dangerous websites that can be used in SmartScreen Filter website checks.

INTERNET OPTIONS

Most people don't realize the scope covered by the Internet Options applet. The settings configured under Internet Options apply not only to Internet Explorer, but also to the operating system. They are systemwide. You can use the Internet Options applet to configure general security settings for any

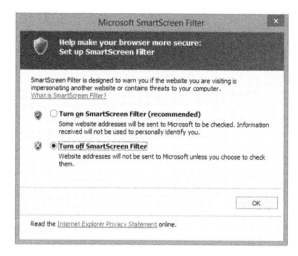

FIGURE 5.10 SmartScreen Filter Window

FIGURE 5.11 Report a Website Screen

application that accesses the Internet. Individual applications may have their own specific settings in addition to these. Internet Options contains both usability configuration items and security-related items. We will focus on the security-related items. The Internet Options applet contains seven tabs: General, Security, Privacy, Content, Connections, Programs, and Advanced.

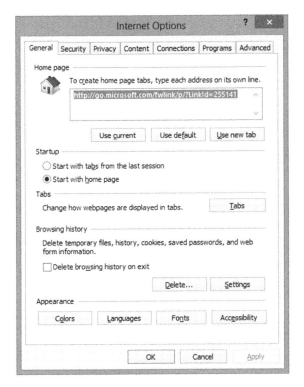

FIGURE 5.12 Internet Options General Tab

General

The General tab of Internet Options, as seen in Figure 5.12, provides functionality for configuring basic Internet Explorer settings. When dealing with security, the two important sections here are Home page and Browsing history.

Home Page

Off hand, you might not see how the home page selection would have security implications. Consider this. A lot of browser-related viruses, worms, etc., will modify your home page. They may point you to a malicious website. Or they may point you to a page on your system that they have modified with malicious code. The malicious site or page may be used to transmit data from your system to a malicious site. In some cases, you may think you have cleaned your system from infections, and the malicious site or page may be used to re-infect your system. Whenever you open your web browser, you will immediately be sent to your home page. So, if you think your system may be infected, you should be sure to check your home page setting. If your home page turns out to be something unexpected, this would be an indicator that you need to investigate your system.

Browsing History

As you use your web browser to navigate through the Internet, certain information is stored on your system. Collectively, this information is called your browsing history. This information is gathered in an effort to improve your browsing experience. Your browsing history can be used to determine a lot of information about you. It can be used to figure out what sites you visit, how often you go to those sites, and in some cases, what you do on those sites. With the proper configuration you can limit what someone can find out about your browsing habits, even if they were to gain physical access to your system.

You have two choices, you can manually delete your browsing history, or you can have Internet Explorer delete it for you. If you select the option for *Delete browsing history on exit*, then every time you close Internet Explorer, your browsing history will automatically be cleared. Otherwise, you have to manually clear out your browsing history. We will go over that shortly.

There are two additional options available in the Browsing History section: Delete and Settings.

Settings

If you click on the Settings button, it will bring up the Website Data Settings window as seen in Figure 5.13. The Website Data Settings has three tabs: Temporary Internet Files, History, and Caches and databases.

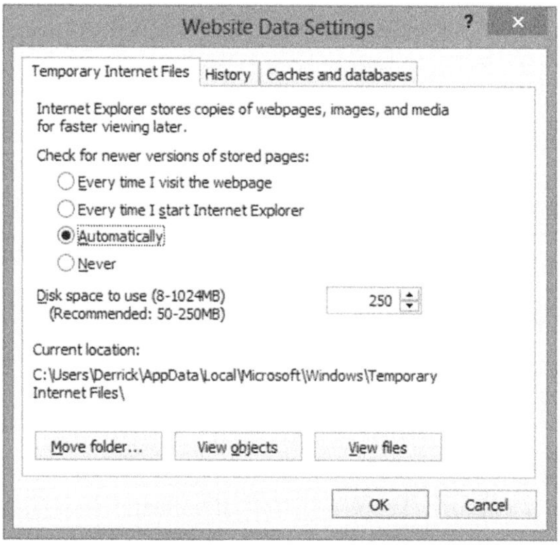

FIGURE 5.13 Website Data Settings Window

Temporary Internet Files. As you go to different websites, Internet Explorer will store files on your system like webpages and images. These files make it easier to view the website. When Internet Explorer visits a website, all cacheable content will be downloaded to the system. It will first be downloaded into memory and then subsequently copied to disk. When you move between pages on a site, Internet Explorer will attempt to read the content from cache before downloading it again. This helps to speed up the browsing process.

There are also a few issues with caching content. These files can be used by an attacker to determine what websites an individual has visited. Also, certain content that you may want to keep private may also be downloaded. There are also instances where downloaded files may be corrupted and causing websites to show up improperly or not show up at all.

Eventually the pages and the files on the website will change. When this happens, you will want to make sure your browser has the newest files, so you aren't seeing stale or out-of-date content. Internet Explorer allows you to configure how often your browser will check for these newer files. You have four options:

- Every time I visit the webpage.
- Every time I start Internet Explorer.
- Automatically.
- Never.

As more and more files are stored on your system, they will take up more and more space. Internet Explorer allows you to configure how much space these temporary files are allowed to take up. You can configure this here. You can also change the location of the temporary files. Perhaps you want them to be stored on a separate drive. Select the Move folder button to change the location of your temporary files.

If you click the View Objects button, it will bring up the Downloaded Program Files folder.

If you look here, you can see whether objects have been installed that you did not intend. Having objects here that you are unaware of can be a sign that your system has been compromised.

If you click the View files button, you will be taken to the Temporary Internet Files folder where the temporary Internet files are stored. In this folder, you can see what files have been downloaded and what Internet cookies have been set on your system. You can also delete individual files and cookies instead of deleting all of them.

History. Internet Explorer keeps a listing of websites you visit. This is called your browser history. Internet Explorer allows you to configure whether it will keep track of this list and how many sites to keep in the list. This list generally

FIGURE 5.14 Website Data Settings History Tab

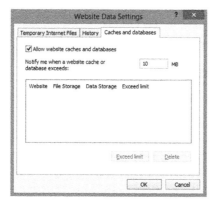

FIGURE 5.15 Website Data Settings—Caches and Databases Tab

shows up in the URL bar. On the History tab, as seen in Figure 5.14, you can configure how many days of history Internet Explorer will keep. If you select 0, then Internet Explorer will not keep track of your browser history.

Caches and Databases. Internet Explorer will let you store application cache and indexed database caches on the local system. The Caches and databases tab, as seen in Figure 5.15, allows you to enable this caching and set a limit on how much can be cached.

Delete

If you click the Delete button on the Internet Options General tab, the Delete Browsing History window appears, as seen in Figure 5.16. Here you can manually delete different types of browsing information stored on your system.

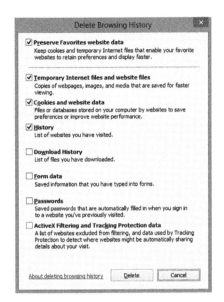

FIGURE 5.16 Delete Browsing History Window

The options are as follows:

- *Preserve Favorites website data:* Selecting this option will preserve website data associated with the websites listed in your favorites.
- *Temporary Internet files and website files:* Selecting this option will cause all the webpages and files that have been copied to your system to be deleted.
- *Cookies and website data:* Selecting this option will cause all the cookies, files, or databases that have been stored on your system to be removed. Although cookies are stored with temporary Internet files, you can delete the two separately. This is because you may want to delete outdated files, but keep your cookies, so that your website preferences and settings are maintained.
- *History:* Selecting this option will cause the history list kept by Internet Explorer to be cleared out.
- *Download History:* Selecting this option will clear out the list of files you have downloaded.
- *Form data:* Selecting this option will clear out data that has been saved regarding forms you have submitted online.
- *Passwords:* Selecting this option will delete stored passwords you have saved for various web forms.
- *ActiveX Filtering and Tracking Protection data:* Selecting this option will delete the list of websites you have excluded from filtering. It will also delete any stored data used by the Tracking Protection feature.

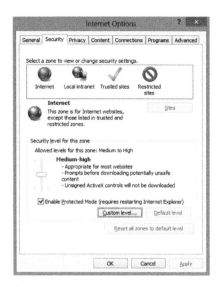

FIGURE 5.17 Internet Options Security Tab

Security

Not all websites need to have the same level of security. But, you probably don't want to have to configure individual settings for every website you visit. Instead you can group different websites into categories and configure settings for each category. In Windows, these categories are called zones. Windows considers four main zones, as seen in Figure 5.17: the Internet zone, the local intranet zone, Trusted sites, and Restricted sites.

Each of these zones represents a trust level. This trust level is accompanied by security settings. Each zone has different default security settings, but they can be changed by clicking the Custom level button. This will bring up the Security Settings window as seen in Figure 5.18. Here you can manually configure each individual setting. You can also reset the settings to a desired security level.

What we will do next is to go through all of the available settings giving a description of each. Then I will outline the default settings for each zone.

Security Settings

Internet Explorer has a feature called protected mode. Protected mode can be set for different security zones. Protected mode helps prevent malicious software from being installed on your system. In Protected Mode, Internet Explorer runs with a reduced set of privileges. With this reduced set of privileges, malicious websites will have a limited ability to interact with the system. There will be restriction on installing or executing code and accessing system data.

FIGURE 5.18 Internet Options Security Settings

Protected mode is enabled by default for all sites, except those in the local intranet.

When in protected mode, Internet Explorer will warn you whenever a website attempts to install software on your system. Internet Explorer will also warn you when a web tries to run software already installed on your system.

On the Security Tab, you also have the option to Reset all zones to default level. This will reset all your security zones back to default levels. This comes in handy if you have made changes that are causing unexpected behaviors. Now we'll go through all the security settings and their available options.

.NET Framework

Loose XAML—Loose XAML is used for content rendering. It is a mark-up only language. This option determines whether Internet Explorer can use loose XAML files. Loose XAML files with code in them can be executed in the browser without being compiled first:

> Disable.
> Enable.
> Prompt.

XAML browser applications—This option allows for executing Windows Presentation Foundation applications in your web browser:

> Disable.
> Enable.
> Prompt.

XPS documents—XPS is the XML paper specification. It is used for printing documents. XPS documents are fairly safe because they don't execute code:

Disable.
Enable.
Prompt.

.NET Framework-Reliant Components

Permissions for components with manifests—This option applies to a feature in the .Net Framework that allows you to add a one click manifest to a control in a browser:

Disable.
High Safety.

Run components not signed with Authenticode—Internet Explorer will check to see if a control is signed with an Authenticode signature. This option determines whether one is required in order to run the object:

Disable.
Enable.
Prompt.

Run components signed with Authenticode—Internet Explorer will check to see if a control is signed with an Authenticode signature. This option determines whether the object is allowed to execute if it is signed:

Disable.
Enable.
Prompt.

ActiveX Controls and Plug-Ins

Allow ActiveX Filtering—ActiveX controls are used to provide additional functionality, but they can also be dangerous. ActiveX Filtering allows you to browse the Internet without using ActiveX controls:

Disable.
Enable.

Allow previously unused ActiveX controls to run without prompt—If you have already used an ActiveX control, Internet Explorer can automatically allow that control the next time it tries to execute:

Disable.
Enable.

Allow Scriptlets—Scriptlets aren't used much today. For the most part, they have been phased out. But, they are still used in some websites. Scriptlets enhance webpages using programming languages:

Disable.
Enable.
Prompt.

Automatic prompting for ActiveX controls—Internet Explorer has an Information Bar (usually yellow) that will allow you to choose what to do when you encounter an ActiveX control and other options for a particular site. If you enable this setting, the bar won't be used for ActiveX controls, you will be prompted to either download or install an ActiveX control:

Disable.
Enable.

Binary and script behaviors—Behaviors are compiled HTML, COM components, or Windows Script components. Allowing these to execute can be dangerous:

Administrator approved.
Disable.
Enable.

Display video and animation on a webpage that does use external media player—This option controls whether you can play media embedded in a webpage:

Disable.
Enable.

Download signed ActiveX controls—This setting deals with whether ActiveX must be signed using a trusted code signing certificate:

Disable.
Enable (not secure).
Prompt (recommended).

Download unsigned ActiveX controls—This setting deals with whether ActiveX must be signed using a trusted code signing certificate:

Disable (recommended).
Enable (recommended).
Prompt.

Initialize and script ActiveX controls not marked as safe for scripting—When ActiveX controls are built, they can be developed in a way where they will be marked as safe scripting. This indicates that limitations have been placed on how the ActiveX control may execute. This option determines whether ActiveX controls not marked safe can still be scripted:

Disable (recommended).
Enable (not secure).
Prompt.

Only allow approved domains to use ActiveX without prompt—This setting controls whether you are prompted when an attempt to activate an ActiveX control is made by a site that did install the ActiveX control:

Disable.
Enable.

Run ActiveX controls and plug-ins—This option controls whether ActiveX controls and plug-ins can be run:

Administrator approved.
Disable.
Enable.
Prompt.

Script ActiveX controls marked safe for scripting—When ActiveX controls are built, they can be developed in a way where they will be marked as safe scripting. This indicates that limitations have been placed on how the ActiveX control may execute. This option determines whether ActiveX controls marked safe can be scripted:

Disable.
Enable.
Prompt.

Downloads
File download—This setting determines whether files can be downloaded. You have to be careful with this setting because the zone is determined by the site where the download link occurs, not by the site where the file is downloaded from:

Disable.
Enable.

Font download—This setting determines whether HTML fonts can be downloaded:

Disable.
Enable.
Prompt.

Enable .NET Framework setup—This setting controls whether a website can launch the .NET Framework setup if needed:

Disable.
Enable.

Miscellaneous

Access data sources across domains—This setting controls whether data can be accessed from another security zone. This access is usually done via MSXML or ADO:

Disable.
Enable.
Prompt.

Allow dragging of content between domains into separate windows—This setting controls whether you can drag and drop content from one domain to another if they are in a separate window:

Disable.
Enable.

Allow dragging of content between domains into the same window—This setting controls whether you can drag and drop content from one domain to another if they are in the same window:

Disable.
Enable.

Allow META REFRESH—This option controls the use of the META REFRESH tab. The META REFRESH tab allows for a webpage to be automatically refreshed after a given interval. It can also be used to direct the browser to another webpage:

Disable.
Enable.

Allow scripting of Microsoft web browser control—This setting determines whether a webpage can control embedded web browser controls via script:

Disable.
Enable.

Allow script-initiated windows without size or position constraints—This setting allows you to control pop-up windows. Hidden pop-up windows are often used to execute malicious code:

Disable.
Enable.

Allow webpages to use restricted protocols for active content—This setting controls whether a protocol restricted in a particular zone can execute scripts and other active content:

Disable.
Enable.
Prompt.

Allow websites to open windows without address or status bars—This option controls whether address or status bars are required when a website opens a window. Without an address bar, you may not know what website is actually being accessed in the window:

Disable.
Enable.

Display mixed content—This option controls whether webpages that contain both secure and nonsecure items can be displayed. Secure items are generally those access via HTTPS:

Disable.
Enable.
Prompt.

Don't prompt for client certificate selection when no certificates or only one certificate exists—Client certificates can be used to authenticate to websites. This option determines whether the client certificate will automatically be sent if you only have one. Otherwise; you will be prompted to submit the certificate:

Disable.
Enable.

Drag and drop or copy and paste files—This option controls whether you can drag and drop from within webpages:

Disable.
Enable.
Prompt.

Enable MIME Sniffing—This is a technique used to determine appropriate content type in webpages.

Disable.
Enable.

Include local directory path when uploading files to a server—This controls whether local path information will be sent to a server when uploading a file.

There is chance that sensitive information could be included in the path. For example, if the local path was a user home directory, it might include the username in the path:

> Disable.
> Enable.

Launching applications and unsafe files—This option controls whether a security warning is displayed when attempting to launch executables:

> Disable.
> Enable.
> Prompt.

Launching programs and files in an IFRAME—This option controls whether programs can be run or files downloaded from an IFRAME:

> Disable.
> Enable (not secure).
> Prompt (recommended).

Navigate windows and frames across different domains—This setting controls whether windows and frames can be opened in a different domain:

> Disable.
> Enable.
> Prompt.

Render legacy filters—This option controls whether legacy visual filters can be rendered:

> Disable.
> Enable.

Submit non-encrypted form data—This option controls whether data in web-based forms has to be encrypted:

> Disable.
> Enable.
> Prompt.

Use Pop-up Blocker—This option controls whether the Pop-up Blocker will be enabled:

> Disable.
> Enable.

Use SmartScreen Filter—This option controls whether SmartScreen Filter will be enabled:

Disable.
Enable.

Userdata persistence—This option controls whether online forms can save a portion of your user information into a file on the disk:

Disable.
Enable.

Websites in less privileged web content zone can navigate into this zone—This option controls whether a website in a more restricted zone can open a window or link to website in this zone:

Disable.
Enable.
Prompt.

Scripting

Active scripting—This option controls whether JavaScript, VBScript, and other scripting languages can be run on a webpage:

Disable.
Enable.
Prompt.

Allow Programmatic clipboard access—This option controls whether websites can access the clipboard:

Disable.
Enable.
Prompt.

Allow status bar updates via script—This option is used to control whether websites can update the status bar:

Disable.
Enable.

Allow websites to prompt for information using scripted windows—This option controls whether a website can use script to display a window that asks\ for user input:

Disable.
Enable.

Enable XSS filter—This option enables the cross-site scripting filter:

Disable.
Enable.

Scripting of Java applets—This option controls whether scripts can access Java applets:

Disable.
Enable.
Prompt.

User Authentication

Logon—This option controls whether logon information can be automatically submitted to websites:

Anonymous logon.
Automatic logon only in Intranet zone.
Automatic logon with current username and password.
Prompt for username and password.

Internet Zone

The Internet zone can be considered the default zone. Websites that do not fall into other zone are automatically considered part of the Internet zone. This is the zone that most of the websites you visit on the Internet will fall under. This zone is second least trusted zone.

Default Security Settings

By default, the settings under the Internet zone are configured for Medium-High security. The individual settings are as follows.

.NET Framework:

Loose XAML—Disable.
XAML browser applications—Disable.
XPS documents—Enable.

.NET Framework-reliant components:

Permissions for components with manifests—High Safety.
Run components not signed with Authenticode—Enable.
Run components signed with Authenticode—Enable.

ActiveX controls and plug-ins:

Allow ActiveX Filtering—Enable.
Allow previously unused ActiveX controls to run without prompt—Disable.

Allow Scriptlets—Disable.
Automatic prompting for ActiveX controls—Disable.
Binary and script behaviors—Enable.
Display video and animation on a webpage that does use external media player—Disable.
Download signed ActiveX controls—Prompt.
Download unsigned ActiveX controls—Disable.
Initialize and script ActiveX controls not marked as safe for scripting—Disable.
Only allow approved domains to use ActiveX without prompt—Enable.
Run ActiveX controls and plug-ins—Enable.
Script ActiveX controls marked safe for scripting—Enable.

Downloads:

File download—Enable.
Font download—Enable.

Enable .NET Framework setup—Enable.

Miscellaneous:
Access data sources across domains—Disable.
Allow dragging of content between domains into separate windows—Disable.
Allow dragging of content between domains into the same window—Disable.
Allow META REFRESH—Enable.
Allow scripting of Microsoft web browser control—Disable.
Allow script-initiated windows without size or position constraints—Disable.
Allow webpages to use restricted protocols for active content—Prompt.
Allow websites to open windows without address or status bars—Disable.
Display mixed content—Prompt.
Don't prompt for client certificate selection when no certificates or only one certificate exists—Disable.
Drag and drop or copy and paste files—Enable.
Enable MIME sniffing—Enable.
Include local directory path when uploading files to a server—Disable.
Launching applications and unsafe files—Prompt.
Launching programs and files in an IFRAME—Prompt.
Navigate windows and frames across different domains—Disable.
Render legacy filters—Disable.
Submit non-encrypted form data—Enable.
Use Pop-up Blocker—Enable.

Use SmartScreen Filter—Enable.
Userdata persistence—Enable.
Websites in less privileged web content zone can navigate into this zone—Enable.

Scripting:

Active scripting—Enable.
Allow Programmatic clipboard access—Prompt.
Allow status bar updates via script—Disable.
Allow websites to prompt for information using scripted windows—Disable.
Enable XSS filter—Enable.
Scripting of Java applets—Enable.

User Authentication:
Logon—Automatic logon only in Intranet zone.

Adding Sites to the Internet Zone

Sites cannot be manually added to the Internet zone. The Internet zone is basically a "catch all" for sites that do not fall into any other zone. This is why you have to be careful when you set permissions for this zone. It's the zone where most websites will fall.

Local Intranet Zone

The Local intranet zone is general for sites on your local network. The Local intranet zone is the second most trusted zone. The idea behind this is that you are generally safe from being attacked by other machines on your local network. That may have been the case a while ago, but nowadays, people often access the Internet on public networks, like at a local coffee house. In these cases, you cannot trust the other systems on the local network. So, you have to be more careful with the settings you set in the Local intranet zone.

Default Security Settings

By default, the settings under the local Intranet zone are configured for Medium security. The individual settings are as follows.

.NET Framework:

Loose XAML—Enable.
XAML browser applications—Enable.
XPS documents—Enable.

.NET Framework-reliant components:

Permissions for components with manifests—High Safety.
Run components not signed with Authenticode—Enable.
Run components signed with Authenticode—Enable.

ActiveX controls and plug-ins:

Allow ActiveX Filtering—Disable.
Allow previously unused ActiveX controls to run without
prompt—Enable.
Allow Scriptlets—Enable.
Automatic prompting for ActiveX controls—Enable.
Binary and script behaviors—Enable.
Display video and animation on a webpage that does use external media
player—Disable.
Download signed ActiveX controls—Prompt.
Download unsigned ActiveX controls—Disable.
Initialize and script ActiveX controls not marked as safe for
scripting—Disable.
Only allow approved domains to use ActiveX without prompt—Disable.
Run ActiveX controls and plug-ins—Enable.
Script ActiveX controls marked safe for scripting—Enable.

Downloads:

File download—Enable.
Font download—Enable.

Enable .NET Framework setup—Enable.

Miscellaneous:

Access data sources across domains—Prompt.
Allow dragging of content between domains into separate
windows—Disable.
Allow dragging of content between domains into the same
window—Disable.
Allow META REFRESH—Enable.
Allow scripting of Microsoft web browser control—Enable.
Allow script-initiated windows without size or position
constraints—Enable.
Allow webpages to use restricted protocols for active content—Prompt.
Allow websites to open windows without address or status bars—Enable.
Display mixed content—Prompt.

Don't prompt for client certificate selection when no certificates or only one certificate exists—Enable.

Drag and drop or copy and paste files—Enable.

Enable MIME sniffing—Enable.

Include local directory path when uploading files to a server—Enable.

Launching applications and unsafe files—Enable.

Launching programs and files in an IFRAME—Prompt.

Navigate windows and frames across different domains—Enable.

Render legacy filters—Enable.

Submit non-encrypted form data—Enable.

Use Pop-up Blocker—Disable.

Use SmartScreen Filter—Disable.

Userdata persistence—Enable.

Websites in less privileged web content zone can navigate into this zone—Enable.

Scripting:

Active scripting—Enable.

Allow Programmatic clipboard access—Enable.

Allow status bar updates via script—Enable.

Allow websites to prompt for information using scripted windows—Enable.

Enable XSS filter—Disable.

Scripting of Java applets—Enable.

User Authentication:

Logon—Automatic logon only in Intranet zone.

Adding Sites to Zone

Generally, any site that you access via a NetBIOS name will be considered part of the Local intranet zone. You can also manually add sites to the zone, by clicking on the Sites button. This will bring up the Local intranet window as seen in Figure 5.19.

The Local intranet window lets you configure rules for which sites will be placed in the local intranet zone. If you select Automatically detect intranet network, Internet Explorer will determine the rules for you. If you deselect that option, you can configure three rules: Include all local (intranet) sites not listed in other zones, Include all sites that bypass the proxy server, and Include all network paths (UNCs).

If you want to manually specify sites, click the Advanced button. It will bring up the Local intranet sites window as shown in Figure 5.20.

FIGURE 5.19 Local Intranet Window

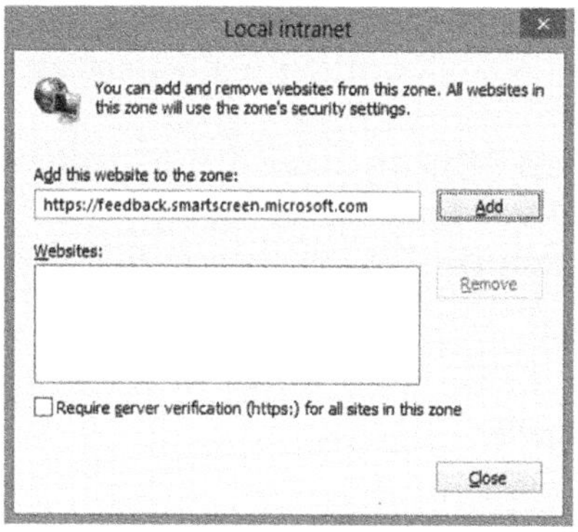

FIGURE 5.20 Local Intranet Sites Window

Trusted Sites

Trusted sites are sites that you trust as being secure. Trusted sites have the least restrictive security settings by default.

Default Security Settings

By default, the settings under the Internet zone are configured for Medium. The individual settings are as follows.

.NET Framework:

> Loose XAML—Enable.
> XAML browser applications—Enable.
> XPS documents—Enable.

.NET Framework-reliant components:

> Permissions for components with manifests—High Safety.
> Run components not signed with Authenticode—Enable.
> Run components signed with Authenticode—Enable.

ActiveX controls and plug-ins:

Allow ActiveX Filtering—Enable.
Allow previously unused ActiveX controls to run without prompt—Enable.
Allow Scriptlets—Disable.
Automatic prompting for ActiveX controls—Disable.
Binary and script behaviors—Enable.
Display video and animation on a webpage that does use external media player—Disable.
Download signed ActiveX controls—Prompt.
Download unsigned ActiveX controls—Disable.
Initialize and script ActiveX controls not marked as safe for scripting—Disable.
Only allow approved domains to use ActiveX without prompt—Disable.
Run ActiveX controls and plug-ins—Enable.
Script ActiveX controls marked safe for scripting—Enable.

Downloads:

File download—Enable.
Font download—Enable.

Enable .NET Framework setup—Enable.

Miscellaneous:

Access data sources across domains—Disable.
Allow dragging of content between domains into separate windows—Disable.
Allow dragging of content between domains into the same window—Disable.
Allow META REFRESH—Enable.
Allow scripting of Microsoft web browser control—Disable.
Allow script-initiated windows without size or position constraints—Disable.
Allow webpages to use restricted protocols for active content—Prompt.
Allow websites to open windows without address or status bars—Enable.
Display mixed content—Prompt.
Don't prompt for client certificate selection when no certificates or only one certificate exists—Disable.
Drag and drop or copy and paste files—Enable.
Enable MIME sniffing—Enable.
Include local directory path when uploading files to a server—Enable.

Launching applications and unsafe files—Prompt.
Launching programs and files in an IFRAME—Prompt.
Navigate windows and frames across different domains—Disable.
Render legacy filters—Enable.
Submit non-encrypted form data—Enable.
Use Pop-up Blocker—Enable.
Use SmartScreen Filter—Enable.
Userdata persistence—Enable.
Websites in less privileged web content zone can navigate into this zone—Enable.

Scripting:

Active scripting—Enable.
Allow Programmatic clipboard access—Prompt.
Allow status bar updates via script—Enable.
Allow websites to prompt for information using scripted windows—Enable.
Enable XSS filter—Enable.
Scripting of Java applets—Enable.

User Authentication:
Logon—Automatic logon only in Intranet zone.

Adding Sites to Zone
Sites must be manually added to the Trusted sites zone. Since the sites here receive the least restrictive permissions, you want to have full cover over which sites end up there. If you click the Sites button, it will bring up the Trusted sites window that you can use to manually add sites.

Restricted Sites
This zone is for sites that are believed to be malicious. Restricted sites have the most restrictive security settings.

Default Security Settings
By default, the settings under the Internet zone are configured for High. The individual settings are as follows.

.NET Framework:

Loose XAML—Disable.
XAML browser applications—Disable.
XPS documents—Disable.

.NET Framework-reliant components:

> Permissions for components with manifests—Disable.
> Run components not signed with Authenticode—Disable.
> Run components signed with Authenticode—Disable.

ActiveX controls and plug-ins:

> Allow ActiveX Filtering—Enable.
> Allow previously unused ActiveX controls to run without prompt—Disable.
> Allow Scriptlets—Disable.
> Automatic prompting for ActiveX controls—Disable.
> Binary and script behaviors—Disable.
> Display video and animation on a webpage that does use external media player—Disable.
> Download signed ActiveX controls—Disable.
> Download unsigned ActiveX controls—Disable.
> Initialize and script ActiveX controls not marked as safe for scripting—Disable.
> Only allow approved domains to use ActiveX without prompt—Enable.
> Run ActiveX controls and plug-ins—Disable.
> Script ActiveX controls marked safe for scripting—Disable.

Downloads:

> File download—Disable.
> Font download—Disable.

Enable .NET Framework setup—Disable.

Miscellaneous:

> Access data sources across domains—Disable.
> Allow dragging of content between domains into separate windows—Disable.
> Allow dragging of content between domains into the same window—Disable.
> Allow META REFRESH—Disable.
> Allow scripting of Microsoft web browser control—Disable.
> Allow script-initiated windows without size or position constraints—Disable.
> Allow webpages to use restricted protocols for active content—Disable.
> Allow websites to open windows without address or status bars—Disable.
> Display mixed content—Prompt.
> Don't prompt for client certificate selection when no certificates or only one certificate exists—Disable.

Drag and drop or copy and paste files—Prompt.

Enable MIME sniffing—Disable.

Include local directory path when uploading files to a server—Disable.

Launching applications and unsafe files—Disable.

Launching programs and files in an IFRAME—Disable.

Navigate windows and frames across different domains—Disable.

Render legacy filters—Disable.

Submit non-encrypted form data—Prompt.

Use Pop-up Blocker—Enable.

Use SmartScreen Filter—Enable.

Userdata persistence—Disable.

Websites in less privileged web content zone can navigate into this zone—Disable.

Scripting:

Active scripting—Disable.

Allow Programmatic clipboard access—Disable.

Allow status bar updates via script—Disable.

Allow websites to prompt for information using scripted windows—Disable.

Enable XSS filter—Enable.

Scripting of Java applets—Disable.

User Authentication:

Logon—Prompt for username and password.

Adding Sites to Zone

Sites must be manually added to the Restricted sites zone. If you click Sites, it will bring up the Restricted sites window that you can use to add sites to the zone.

Privacy

The Privacy tab of Internet Options allows you to control how much information websites can track and store about your system. You can configure cookie settings, location services, Pop-up Blocker, and InPrivate Browsing.

Settings

The Settings section is where you configure cookie settings for sites that fall within the Internet zone. There are six preconfigured settings available here:

- *Block All Cookies:* Blocks all cookies from all websites. Cookies that are already on this computer cannot be read by websites.

- *High:* Blocks all cookies from websites that do not have a compact privacy policy. Blocks cookies that save information that can be used to contact you without your explicit consent.
- *Medium High:* Blocks third-party cookies that do not have a compact privacy policy. Blocks third-party cookies that save information that can be used to contact you without your explicit consent. Blocks first-party cookies that save information that can be used to contact you without your implicit consent.
- *Medium:* Blocks third-party cookies that do not have a compact privacy policy. Blocks third-party cookies that save information that can be used to contact you without your explicit consent. Restricts first-party cookies that save information that can be used to contact you without your implicit consent.
- *Low:* Blocks third-party cookies that do not have a compact privacy policy. Restricts third-party cookies that save information that can be used to contact you without your implicit consent.
- *Accept All Cookies:* Save cookies from any website. Cookies that are already on this computer can be read by the websites that created them.

Clicking the Sites button will bring up the Per Site Privacy Actions window as seen in Figure 5.21. Here you can add cookie settings for specific sites. The settings are a little limited. You can either always allow cookies for a site or always deny cookies for the site.

Clicking the Import button will bring up the Privacy Import window. You will be able to select a set of Internet privacy preferences to import.

FIGURE 5.21 Per Site Privacy Actions Window

FIGURE 5.22 Advanced Privacy Settings Window

Clicking the Advanced button will bring up the Advanced Privacy Settings window as seen in Figure 5.22. You can override the automatic cookie handling settings. You can configure settings for first-party and third-party cookies. You can also configure whether session cookies will be allowed.

Clicking the Default button will reset the settings back to the default setting of Medium. It provides a balance of security and usability. Many websites require cookies to function properly. So it's important that you understand the nature of the websites that will be visited, before changing the settings.

Location
The Location section allows you to control whether websites are allowed to access the physical location of your system. To start, your system must have some means of tracking your physical location. This is generally done through a connection to a WiFi, cellular, or GPS network. You can block sites from being able to access this information. Also, if there are sites that you have previously allowed to access your location information, you can also block them.

Pop-Up Blocker
The Pop-up Blocker section allows you to prevent browser pop-ups from appearing on your system. If you select the option for Turn on Pop-up Blocker, you can then click the Settings button and configure your Pop-up Blocker settings. After clicking the Settings button, the Pop-up Blocker Settings window, as seen in Figure 5.23, will appear.

Exceptions. The Exceptions section allows you to manually configure exceptions for particular sites. Pop-ups will be allowed on the sites you configure here.

Notifications and Blocking Level. The Notifications and blocking level section enables you to configure what will happen when a pop-up is blocked. You can also configure the blocking level you would like to use.

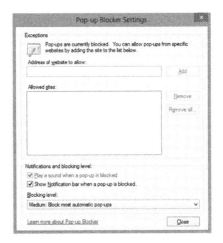

FIGURE 5.23 Pop-Up Blocker Settings Window

Your notification options are as follows:

■ Play a sound when a pop-up is blocked. (Make sure sound is on.)
■ Show Information Bar when a pop-up is blocked.

You can configure your system for one of three blocking levels:

High: Block all pop-ups (Ctrl+Alt to override).
Medium: Block most automatic pop-ups.
Low: Allow pop-ups from secure sites.

InPrivate

InPrivate Browsing attempts to hide your browsing habits for websites and other users on the system. Sometimes different toolbars and extensions can also be used to track this information. This option helps you to prevent this from happening. Just click the option for Disable toolbars and extensions when InPrivate Browsing starts.

Content

The Content tab is used to manage how content is handled by your system. You can configure who can access certain types of content and what they can do with the content. We will cover the Certificates and AutoComplete sections.

Certificates

The Certificates section is used to manage digital certificates. Digital certificates can be used for authentication and encryption. The Certificates section has three options: Clear SSL state, Certificates, and Publishers.

Clear SSL State

When you authenticate to a system using an SSL client certificate, that certificate is stored in cache. The Clear SSL state button is used to clear the SSL cache on the system. Simply click the button the cache will be cleared.

Certificates

The Certificates option is used to manage digital certificates on the system. Clicking the Certificates button will bring up the Certificates applet as seen in Figure 5.24. Here you can view and manage your personal certificates, other people's certificates, intermediate certificate authorities, trusted root certificate authorities, trusted publishers, and untrusted publishers.

Publishers

A developer may use a code signing certificate to sign code so that users know where the code originated. Publishers are trusted authorities that issue signing certificates. If you click the Publishers button, it will bring up the Certificate applet, but on the Trusted publishers tab.

AutoComplete

The AutoComplete feature allows Internet Explorer to automatically fill in forms on websites based on information you have previously entered. If you click the Settings buttons it will bring up the AutoComplete Settings window as seen in Figure 5.25.

AutoComplete can be used in the address bar for browsing history, favorites, feeds, Windows Search, and suggesting URLs. It can also be used to fill out web-based forms. You have an additional option for saving and submitting usernames and passwords on forms. If you choose the Manage Passwords

FIGURE 5.24 Certificates Applet

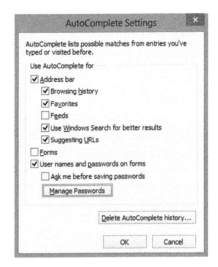

FIGURE 5.25 AutoComplete Settings Window

button, it will bring up Credential Manager, as seen in Figure 5.26. Credential Manager is used to store Web and Windows credentials.

You also have the option for Delete AutoComplete history. If you click this button, it will bring up the Delete Browsing History window, where you can select to delete various components of your browsing history, including those set by AutoComplete.

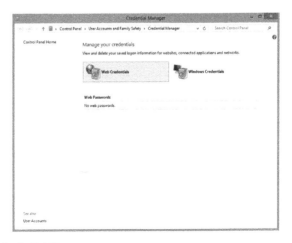

FIGURE 5.26 Credential Manager

Connections

The Connections tab allows you to configure settings for making network and Internet connections. You can configure dial-up connections, VPN connections, and proxy server connections. We will cover configuring proxy settings.

Local Area Network (LAN) Settings

The Local Area Network (LAN) settings section is where you configure your proxy server settings. If you click the LAN settings button, it will bring up the Local Area Network (LAN) Settings window, as seen in Figure 5.27. This is where you can configure your proxy server settings.

There are two choices for automatically configuring your proxy settings:

- *Automatically detect settings.*
- *Use automatic configuration script*—If you choose this option, you will have to enter the location of a configuration file, such as a pac file.

In the Proxy Server section, you can configure the address and port for your proxy server. You can use an IP address or an FQDN. Your connections will automatically be forwarded to the server specified. You also have the option to bypass proxy server for local addresses. If your system believes the remote system is on your local network, based on name or IP address, the system will attempt to make a direct connection, instead of going through the proxy server.

If you click the button for Advanced, it will bring up the Proxy Settings window, as seen in Figure 5.28. Here you can configure different proxy servers or ports for different types of proxying. You can configure HTTP, Secure, FTP, or Socks proxies. In the Proxy Settings window, you also have the option to configure proxy exceptions. When you attempt to access any of the addresses entered here, your system will automatically bypass the proxy server. You can

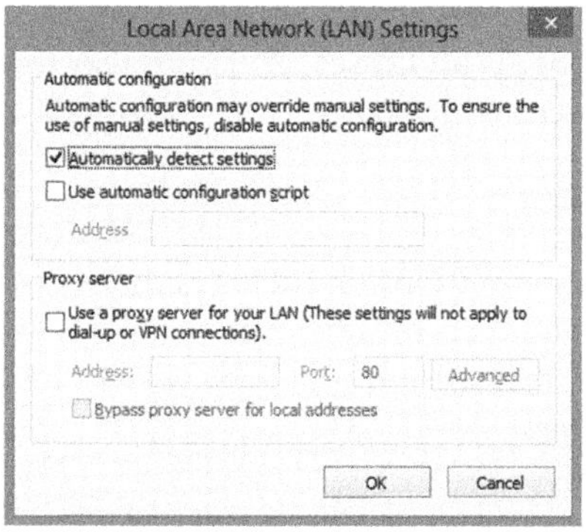

FIGURE 5.27 Local Area Network Settings Window

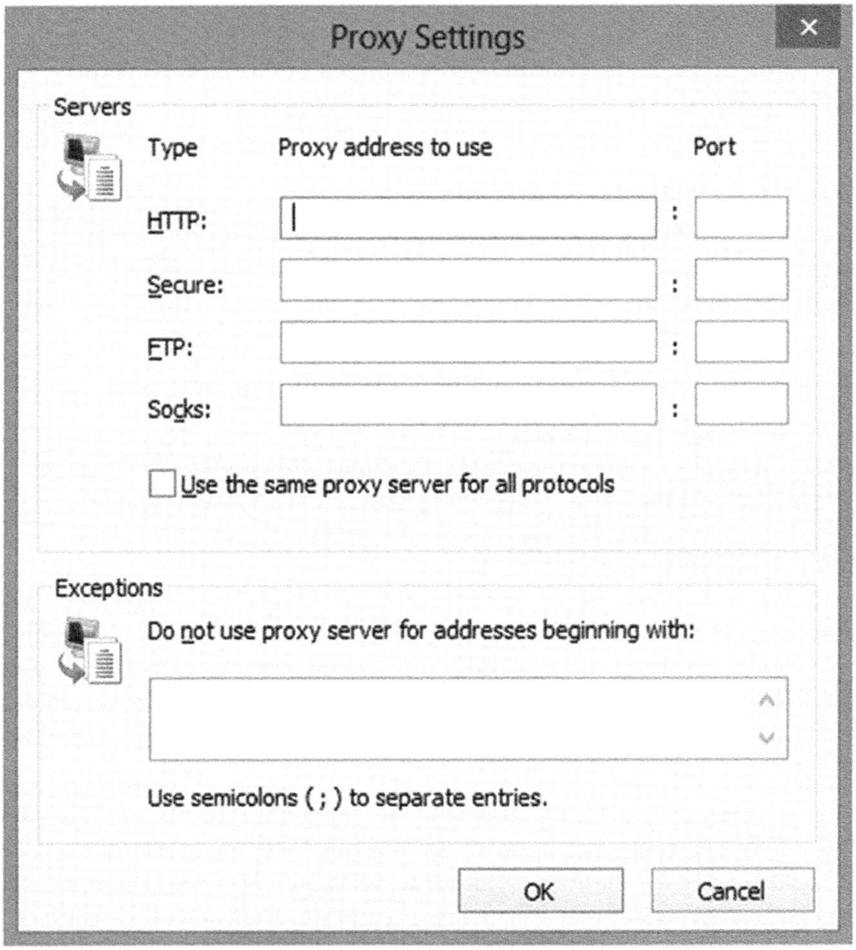

FIGURE 5.28 Proxy Settings Window

enter domain names or IP addresses. You can also use wildcards to specify ranges of addresses or entire domains.

Programs

The Programs tab of Internet Option includes many configuration items. You can configure the default web browser, the default HTML editor, and default programs for Internet services. But, the item we will be concerned with is the management of add-ons.

Manage Add-Ons

If you click the button for Manage Add-ons, it will bring up the Manage Add-ons window, as seen in Figure 5.29. There are four types of add-ons you can

FIGURE 5.29 Manage Add-Ons Window

manage: Toolbars and Extensions, Search Providers, Accelerators, and InPrivate Filtering.

Toolbars and Extensions

Toolbars and extensions are the most commonly used types of add-ons. In this section, you will see information about all of the add-ons that have been installed for the user. You can see the add-on name and publisher. You can also see if the add-on is enabled or disabled and how long it takes for the add-on to activate. If you right-click on an add-on and select More information, you can see advanced information about the add-on, as seen in Figure 5.30.

Search Providers

The Search Providers section will show search providers that have been added to the system. You can configure whether the search provider is allowed to make search suggestions and whether the top result will be displayed in the address bar. If you have multiple search providers, they can be listed in order of preference. You can also specify a search provider as your default.

FIGURE 5.30 Add-Ons Additional Information

Accelerators

Accelerators provide additional context-sensitive functionality inside a webpage. You can use them to translate text or map out directions. The Accelerators section allows you to configure accelerators for different categories like email and map. If you have multiple accelerators, you can configure one for the default.

Tracking Protection

When you visit various websites from the same provider, information about your visit may be shared with other sites. Tracking Protection allows you to prevent this from happening. If you enable Tracking Protection, you will need to configure your Personalized Tracking Protection List. After enabling Tracking Protection, you can click the Settings button. This will bring up the Personalized Tracking Protection List as seen in Figure 5.31. This list outlines which sites are allowed to share content and which are blocked from doing so.

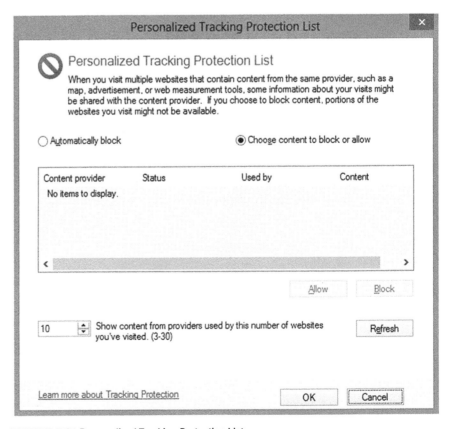

FIGURE 5.31 Personalized Tracking Protection List

Advanced

The Advanced tab is used to configure more advanced Internet settings. Most of these settings are overall settings and do not apply to a particular zone or website.

Settings

The Settings section is where most of the advanced configuration takes. Place I'll list out all the settings and give a brief explanation of each one.

Browsing:

> Automatically recover from page layout errors with Compatibility View.
> Disable script debugging (Internet Explorer).
> Disable script debugging (Other).
> Display a notification about every script error.
> Enable automatic crash recovery.
> Enable third-party browser extensions.
> Show friendly HTTP error messages.
> Use inline AutoComplete (outside of Internet Explorer).
> Use Passive FTP.

HTTP 1.1 Settings:

> Use HTTP 1.1.
> Use HTTP 1.1 through proxy connections.

Search from the Address bar:

> Do not submit unknown addresses to your auto-search provider.
> Just display the results in the main window.

Security:

> Allow active content from CDs to run on My Computer.
> Allow active content to run in files on My Computer.
> Allow software to run or install even if the signature is invalid.
> Check for publisher's certificate revocation.
> Check for signatures on downloaded programs.
> Do not save encrypted pages to disk. (see Figures 5.32 and 5.33)
> Empty Temporary Internet Files folder when browser is closed.
> Enable DOM Storage.
> Enable Integrated Windows Authentication.
> Enable memory protection to help mitigate online attacks.
> Enable native XMLHTTP support.
> Enable SmartScreen Filter.

Use SSL 2.0, Use SSL 3.0, Use TLS 1.0, Use TLS 1.1, Use TLS 1.2—SSL and TLS are used to encrypt network traffic. If possible you should only use the newest version, TLS 1.2. For compatibility reasons, you will probably need to enable other versions. But you do need to be careful. For example, there have been successful man-in-the-middle attacks done against SSL 2.0. So, it should be disabled unless you have a specific need for it.

Warn about certificate address mismatch—With this setting, an error will be generated if the name in the certificate is not the same as the name in the URL.

Warn if changing between secure and not secure mode.

Warn if POST submittal is redirected to a zone that does not permit posts.

Resetting Settings

You also have two other options available on the page. They allow you to reset the settings you have configured. They are:

- Restore advanced settings—This option allows you to reset all the options on the Advanced tab back to default.
- Reset—This option will reset all Internet Explorer settings back to default.

CHAPTER 6

Network Diagnostics and Troubleshooting

INFORMATION IN THIS CHAPTER

- Task Manager
- Resource Monitor
- Performance Monitor
- Event Viewer
- Network Monitor

CONTENTS

An important part of network security is networking monitoring and troubleshooting. It's important to be able to identify issues and determine the source of these issues. Now that we've set up and configured your network, we need to learn about some tools for protecting and monitoring it. Windows 8 and Windows Server 2012 systems come with a number of tools that you can use to prevent and detect network issues. The tools we will be covering are Task Manager, Resource Monitor, Performance Monitor, and Event Viewer. We will also make a brief mention of Network Monitor.

TASK MANAGER

Task Manager has been revamped in Windows 8 and Windows Server 2012. Microsoft wanted to cut out the pieces that weren't really being used and expand the pieces that were. When troubleshooting network issues and looking for suspicious network activity, Task Manager can give you valuable network-related information. You can see overall network usage or which processes are taking up an unusual amount of network bandwidth. There are seven tabs available in Task Manager, but we will only be covering six: Processes, Performance, App history, Startup, Users, and Services.

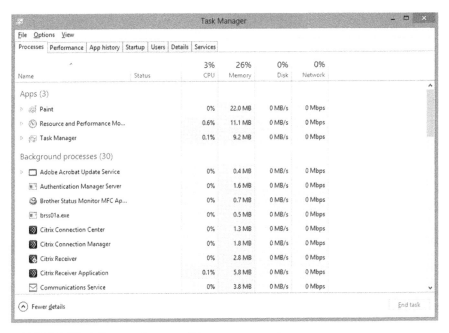

FIGURE 6.1 Task Manager Processes Tab

Processes

The Processes Tab, as seen in Figure 6.1, shows which processes are currently running on the system. You can see the processes that are running and the resources being used by each process. You can look for a few signs here. You can check to see if a network-related process like Internet Explorer is showing excessively high resource utilization. You can also check to see if any process is showing an excessive amount of network utilization. To make finding misbehaving processes easier, Task Manager provides heat map functionality. The heat map uses color coding to show you which processes are using an excessive amount of system's resources.

Task Manager can provide you additional information about the processes you see. If you right-click on a process and select Properties, it will bring up the Properties window, as seen in Figure 6.2. Here, you can see the properties for the process. You can see the path and executable used by the process. You can see if the executable was digitally signed as well as other useful information.

Oftentimes, you may find a process that you do not recognize. If you don't know anything about the process, there is no way for you to be able to tell if the utilization you are seeing for the process is normal. When this happens, you need a way of finding out more information about the process. Task Manager

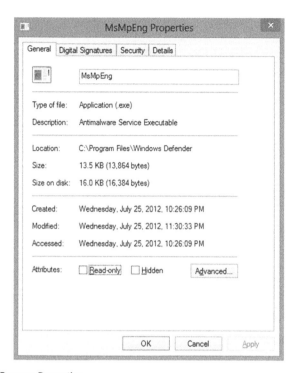

FIGURE 6.2 Process Properties

provides you a simple means for doing this. You can right-click on the process and select Search online. You will then be provided with online search information for the process, as seen in Figure 6.3.

If you want more information about the process to be displayed in the default window, you can add additional columns. If you right-click on the current heading, you will be presented with the column selection menu as seen in Figure 6.4. You can choose to show the following columns: Type, Status, Publisher, PID, Process Name, Command line, CPU, Memory, Disk, and Network.

Performance Tab

On the Performance tab, you can see general system performance information. Of particular interest to us is the network information, as seen in Figure 6.5. You can see information on all of the networks you have configured on your system. You can see IP address, connection type, and SSID if the network is wireless. The most important information shown here is network utilization. You can see how much of the throughput of a given interface is being used. You can see the amount of data sent and the amount of data received.

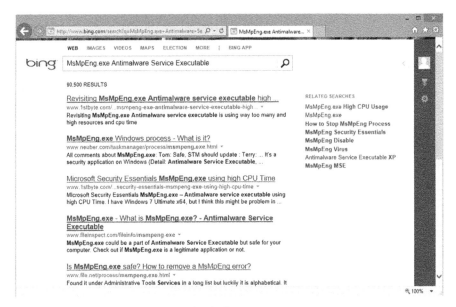

FIGURE 6.3 Task Manager Search Online Option

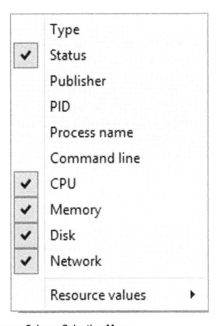

FIGURE 6.4 Task Manager Column Selection Menu

FIGURE 6.5 Task Manager Performance Tab

Property	Ethernet	Wi-Fi	Ethernet	Ethernet
Network utilization	0%	0%	0%	0%
Link speed	100 Mbps	65 Mbps	100 Mbps	100 Mbps
State	Disconnected	Connected	Connected	Connected
Bytes sent throughput	0%	0%	0%	0%
Bytes received throughput	0%	0%	0%	0%
Bytes throughput	0%	0%	0%	0%
Bytes sent	0	174,209	10,166	10,166
Bytes received	0	422,110	0	0
Bytes	0	596,319	10,166	10,166
Bytes sent per interval	0	0	0	0
Bytes received per interval	0	0	0	0
Bytes per interval	0	0	0	0
Unicasts sent	0	1,063	0	0
Unicasts received	0	1,073	0	0
Unicasts	0	2,136	0	0
Unicasts sent per interval	0	0	0	0
Unicasts received per interval	0	0	0	0
Unicasts per interval	0	0	0	0
Nonunicasts sent	0	374	0	0
Nonunicasts received	0	52	62	62
Nonunicasts	0	426	62	62
Nonunicasts sent per interval	0	0	0	0
Nonunicasts received per inter...	0	0	0	0
Nonunicasts per interval	0	0	0	0

FIGURE 6.6 Task Manager Network Details

Task Manager can also provide more detailed network usage information. If you right-click on the throughput graph and select *View network details*, this will bring up the Network Details window, as seen in Figure 6.6. Here you can see

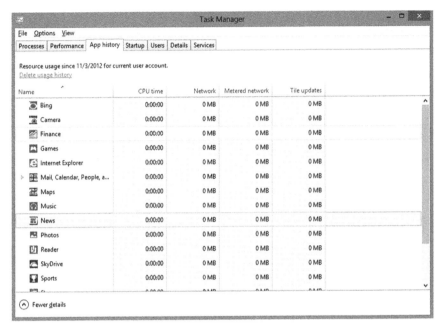

FIGURE 6.7 Task Manager App History Tab

network utilization, bytes sent and received, unicast information, and many other network details.

App History

The App history tab, as seen in Figure 6.7, will display historical resource usage information for each application. You can use it to see how much network bandwidth has been used by an application over time. Some malicious applications don't use a lot of network bandwidth all at once; it's spread out over time. The App history tab can help you detect these applications. The App history tab also includes heat map functionality. The heat map will use color coding to denote applications that have used a large amount of system resources over time.

The time interval used in the App history continues until it is reset. In order to reset the counts, select the option for Delete usage history. The counters will then reset.

Startup

The Startup tab, as seen in Figure 6.8, lists applications that have been designated to start when Windows starts. You should make sure you are familiar with these applications. This way, if an application shows up that shouldn't be there, you will notice.

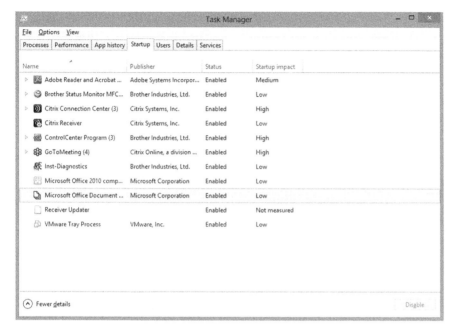

FIGURE 6.8 Task Manager Startup Tab

Users

The Users tab, as seen in Figure 6.9, will show per-user resource utilization. You can see utilization for any user that is logged into the system. You will be able to see if there is an unknown user session logged into the system.

Services

The Services tab, as seen in Figure 6.10, will show all the services installed on the system. You can see whether the service is running or stopped. If it is running, you can see the process ID that it is running under. You also have the options to start, stop, or restart services.

In addition, if you right-click on a running service and choose Go to details, you will be taken to the Details tab of Task Manager where you can see more detailed information about the service and the process running the service.

RESOURCE MONITOR

Resource Monitor can be used for tracking suspicious activity, troubleshooting, or for just figuring out what can be done to fine-tune your system and increase performance. Using Resource Monitor is easy. It can be launched from the

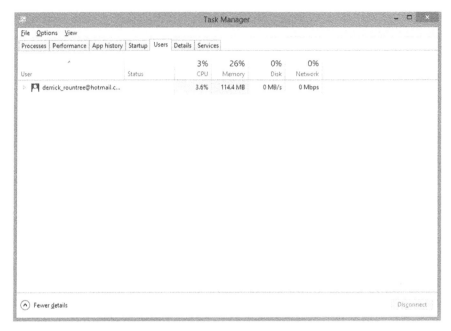

FIGURE 6.9 Task Manager Users Tab

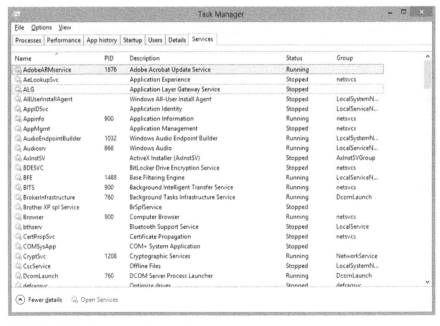

FIGURE 6.10 Task Manager Services Tab

Performance tab in Task Manager or by running **resmon.exe** from the Search programs and files window or the Run window. Resource Monitor will show information about process, services, and certain hardware devices. Throughout Resource Monitor you have the ability to start, stop, and restart process. You also have the ability to suspend processes, resume processes, end processes, and end process trees.

Resource Monitor groups the information it displays in order to make it easier to understand. There are five tabs in Resource Monitor: Overview, CPU, Memory, Disk, and Network. Each tab provides useful information for seeing what's going on with your system. But, we will only be covering the network-related portions of Resource Monitor.

Resource Monitor Overview Tab

The Overview tab of Resource Monitor, as seen in Figure 6.11, gives you a general overview of what is happening in your system. If you want more detailed information than what is given in the sections on the Overview tab, you have to go to the other tabs. There are four sections on the Overview tab—CPU, Disk, Network, and Memory:

- *CPU:* The CPU section of the Overview tab gives information on processes running on the system. You can find out process IDs, number of threads used, CPU consumption, and average percent of CPU consumption. This can help you determine if a process is hogging up the CPU.

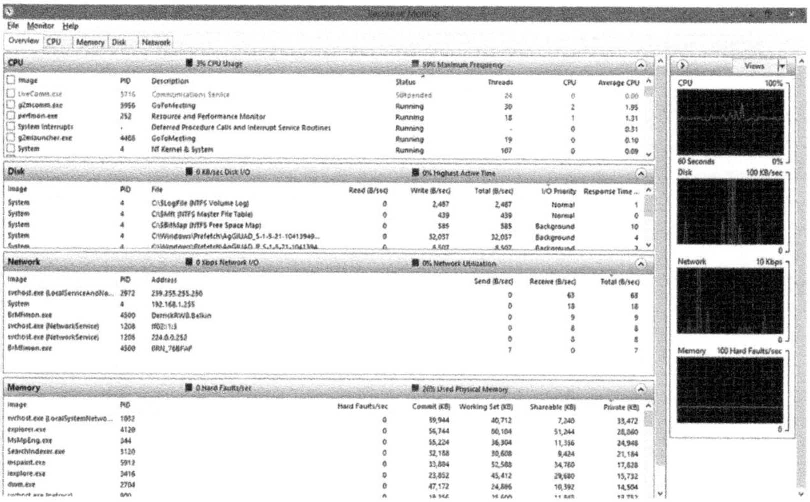

FIGURE 6.11 Resource Monitor—Overview Tab

- *Disk:* The Disk section of the Overview tab gives information on disk activity. You can see which processes are using the disk. You can see read rates and write rates. This can help you determine if a process is causing excessive disk usage.
- *Network:* The Network section of the Overview tab gives information about network activity. It shows processes, the network address they are connected to, bytes sent, and bytes received. This can help you determine if a process is flooding the network.
- *Memory:* The Memory section of the Overview gives information about memory usage on the system. It will tell you the working set and private bytes used by each process. It will also tell you if processes are generating hard faults. You can use this information to tell you if a process is leaking memory or if you need to add memory to your system.

Similar to Task Manager, Resource Monitor has the ability to help you find out information about processes you don't recognize. If you see a process you don't recognize, right-click on it and select Search online. You will then be provided with web search information about the process.

To make it easier to view information about a particular process, Resource Monitor includes an option to do filtering. If you check the box next to the desired process, your view will be filtered for that process, as seen in Figure 6.12.

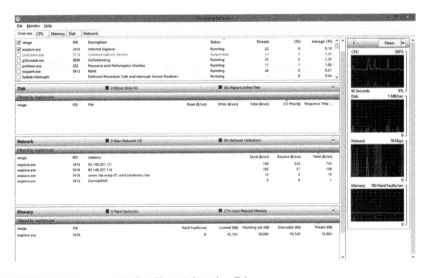

FIGURE 6.12 Resource Monitor Filtered Overview Tab

Resource Monitor Network Tab

The Resource Monitor Network Tab, as seen in Figure 6.13, gives information on network activity on the system. You can view network usage information, connection information, and port information. In the right pane, you can see total network usage, number of TCP connections, local LAN usage, and wireless network usage. This can help you figure out if a network bottleneck is occurring on a specific network or all networks.

The Resource Monitor Network Tab provides detailed information on what's happening with your network connections. You can use this information to troubleshoot connection issues or port conflicts. The Resource Monitor Network Tab has four sections—Processes with Network Activity, Network Activity, TCP Connections, and Listening Ports:

- *Processes with Network Activity:* The Processes with Network Activity section of the Network Tab gives general network activity information. You can see the processes that are running, process ID, bytes sent, bytes received, and total bytes. This can help you determine if a process is generating excess network activity.
- *Network Activity:* The Network Activity section provides the same information that's found in the Network section of the Overview tab. You can see process name, process ID, remote address, sent bytes, received bytes, and total bytes. You can use this information to determine what remote systems your system is communicating with, and how much data is being sent between the two systems.

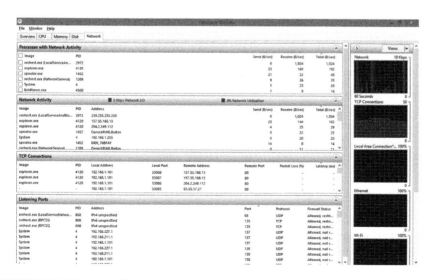

FIGURE 6.13 Resource Monitor—Network Tab

- *TCP Connections:* The TCP Connections section of the Network Tab shows active TCP connections. You can see what remote systems you are connected to and what TCP ports are being used. This section shows process name, process ID, local address and port, remote address and port, packet loss, and latency. The information in this section can help troubleshoot dropped connections, which are often a result of high latency and/or packet loss.
- *Listening Ports:* The Listening Ports section of the Network tab gives you information about the services and processes on your system that are waiting to service network requests. These services are listening on either a TCP or a UDP port. This section shows process name, process ID, listening address, port, protocol, and firewall status. The Listening Port section of the Network tab can come in very handy. It can tell you what ports a given service is listening on. This is very useful if you are trying to figure out why a given service is not accepting requests. It can also help you resolve port conflicts. You may be trying to configure a service to start on a particular port, but keep getting a message about the port being in use. You can use the Listening Ports section to determine what service may be using the port you are trying to configure the new service with.

The Network tab supports the filtering option that allows you to filter based on a specific process. Simply check the box next to the desired process in the Processes with Network Activity section. The Network tab also includes the Search online feature to help make monitoring and troubleshooting easier. Simply right-click on the desired process and select Search online.

PERFORMANCE MONITOR

Performance Monitor, as seen in Figure 6.14, has been around for a long time. It is used to gather performance statistics on your system. You can view statistics in real time or log statistics for future review. Performance Monitor uses performance counters, event trace data, and configuration information settings to determine what to log and monitor. Performance counters show system usage and activity like memory usage, processor usage, etc. Event trace data is taken from trace providers on the OS and in applications. Configuration information specifies which registry keys to pull information from.

Data Collector Sets

Performance Monitor uses Data Collector Sets to group what information to gather. Performance Monitor includes two built-in Data Collector Sets. They are System Diagnostics and System Performance. You can also create your own. You can create a Data Collector Set specific to the network-related information you need to diagnose and troubleshoot issues.

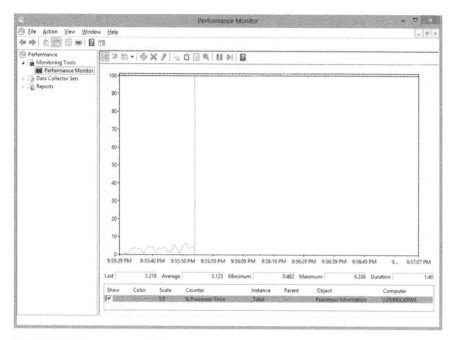

FIGURE 6.14 Performance Monitor

To create your own Data Collector Set, do the following:

1. Under Data Collector Sets, right-click on User Defined and select New > Data Collector Set. This will bring up the Create new Data Collector Set wizard, as seen in Figure 6.15.
2. Give your Data Collector a name, and choose where to create one manually or use a template. We will use a template for this example. Click Next.
3. On the Template Selection screen, as seen in Figure 6.16, choose which template you want to use. For this example, we will use the basic template. Click Next.
4. On the Data Collector Set Storage Location screen, as seen in Figure 6.17, choose where you would like to save Performance Monitor data for the Data Collector Set. Click Next.
5. On the Start New Data Collector Set window, as seen in Figure 6.18, choose the account you want to use to run the Data Collector and whether you want to start the collection now. We will use the default account and start the collection now.

The Data Collector Set will now appear under the User Defined section. You can open the new Data Collector Set to find and edit which Performance Counter, Configuration, and Kernel Trace settings are being used.

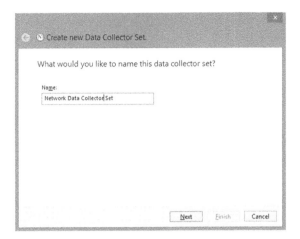

FIGURE 6.15 Create New Data Collector Set Wizard

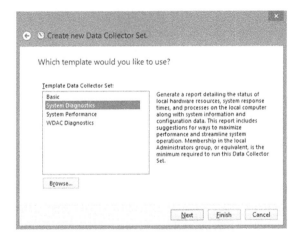

FIGURE 6.16 Performance Monitor Data Collector Set Template

Performance Counters

Performance counters determine what information will be gathered. Performance Monitor includes many counters that will be helpful in troubleshooting your network. Here are a few of the ones that you may find useful:

- .Net CLR Networking;
- .Net CLR Networking 4.0.0.0.0;
- DNS64 Global;
- Generic IKEv1, AuthIP, and IKEv2;
- HTTP Service;
- HTTP Service Request Queues;

FIGURE 6.17 Data Collector Set Storage Location

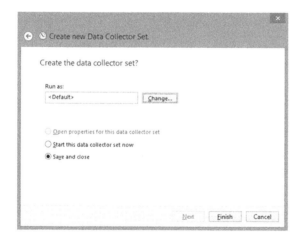

FIGURE 6.18 Start New Data Collector Set Window

- HTTP Service Url Groups;
- ICMP;
- ICMPv6;
- IPHTTPS Global;
- IPHTTPS Session;
- IPSec AuthIP IPv4;
- IPSec AuthIP IPv6;
- IPSec connections;
- IPSec Driver;
- IPSec IKEv1 IPv4;

- IPSec IKEv1 IPv6;
- IPSec IKEv2 IPv4;
- IPSec IKE2 IPv6;
- IPv4;
- IPv6;
- Network Adapter;
- Network Interface;
- Physical Network Interface Card Activity;
- RAS;
- RAS Port;
- RAS Total;
- Server;
- Server Work Queues;
- SMB2 Client Shares;
- SMB2 Server Sessions;
- SMB2 Server Shares;
- TCPv4;
- TCPv6;
- Telephony;
- Terminal Services;
- Terminal Services Session;
- UDPv4;
- UDPv6.

EVENT VIEWER

The Event Viewer is as essential tool for monitoring and logging in Windows systems. You can view user information, application information, and system information. The amount of information that can be collected in Event Viewer can be somewhat overwhelming. This is why it's important to have good understanding of what is logged where, and why. Having this understanding will allow you to better focus your efforts. We will be taking a look at the Windows Logs section and the Applications and Services Logs section.

Windows Logs

The Windows Log section is what most people are used to seeing in a typical Event Viewer session. These logs represent logging for the basic functionalities within Windows. Items logged to the Windows Logs will have the following information associated with them:

- *Level:* This option represents the logging level of the event. It would give information, warning, error, or critical. Critical being the most serious.

- *Keywords:* This is seen in the Security Log. It denotes the type of event logged. It will either be audit success or audit failure.
- *Date and Time:* This is the date and time the event was logged.
- *Source:* This will tell you which module or subsystem reported the information.
- *Event ID:* Each different type of Event Viewer log entry has a different Event ID. This option will help you better understand the nature of the log entry.
- *Task Category:* If there is a task associated with an event log entry, it should be associated with a category. This will help you understand the nature of the entry and a possible cause.

When you open an entry in Event Viewer, you will be taken to the General tab of the Event Properties window, as seen in Figure 6.19. You will be able to see all the general information associated with the event. You will see Log Name, Source, Event ID, Level, User, OpCode, Logged (date and time), Task Category, Keywords, and Computer. You also have the choice to use Online Help to view more information about the entry. Event Viewer will also give you option to copy the contents of the event so it is pasted somewhere else, like an email.

There are five logs in the Windows Logs section—*Application, Security, Setup, System,* and *Forwarded Events*:

- *Application Log:* The Application Log where you can find information about applications that are running on your system. You can find information about Windows 7 applications, other Microsoft applications, and various third-party applications. Application Log is very useful in determining why an application is not functioning properly.
- *Security Log:* The Windows Event Viewer contains a Security Logs section that can be used for security auditing. The Security Log holds auditing

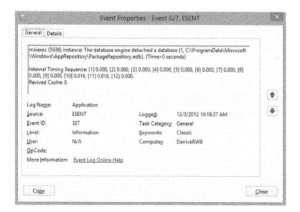

FIGURE 6.19 Event Properties—General Tab

events. You can audit everything from system access to file access. You will see success events and failure events. The Security Log is very useful in trying to determine if someone is trying to gain access to your system. The Security Log can also help you determine if application is trying to access something it does have rights to, or trying to perform a function it does not have right to do. This can be a sign of malicious activity.

- *Setup Log:* The Setup Log is for certain setup and installation events. For example, certain Windows Update initiated installations will be logged.
- *System Log:* The System Log will show events logged by the operating system and Windows services. The System Log can be used to determine what services didn't start and possibly why they didn't start.
- *Forwarded Events:* The Forwarded Events Log allows you to aggregate logs from many different systems into one place. The Forwarded Events Log will show event entries sent to the computer from other computers. This log is disabled by default. In order to receive entries in the Forwarded Events Log, you must enable subscriptions and subscribe to a remote system.

Applications and Services Logs

The Applications and Services Logs are a collection of logs that offer information about specific services and specific applications. These applications and services each have their own log. Simply view the log for the application or service you want more information on. For network-related information you should view the logs under Internet Explorer and the Windows nodes.

Microsoft Windows

The Microsoft node contains a sub-node for Windows. Under here is a large list of Windows applications and services that can be monitored. Here is the list of some of the network-related services that you should consider checking:

- DHcp-client;
- DHcp-Nap-Enforcement-Client;
- DHCPv6-Client;
- DNS Client Events;
- HomeGroup Control Panel;
- HomeGroup Provider Service;
- HomeGroup-Listener Service;
- HttpService;
- Network Access Protection;
- RemoteAssistance;
- RemoteDesktopServices-RdpCoreTS;
- Security-Netlogon;

- SMBClient;
- SMBServer;
- TCPIP;
- WebAuth;
- Windows Firewall With Advanced Security;
- WinHttp;
- Winlogon.

NETWORK MONITOR

Another popular tool that can be downloaded is Network Monitor. We won't be covering Network Monitor in depth, but it is worth mentioning. Microsoft Network Monitor can be downloaded from the Microsoft web site. Network Monitor used to be the premier tool used for network capture and analysis on Windows systems. Network Monitor allows you to capture and examine network traffic flowing through your network. Network Monitor allows you to choose which network interface you want to use to collect network traffic. This is especially useful if your system contains multiple interfaces. Network Monitor also includes a wide variety of parsers and parsing options to filter network traffic to make it easier to capture and examine.

SUMMARY

Windows includes a number of diagnostics and troubleshooting tools to help in detecting network issues. Monitoring your environment will help you track down abnormal activity. You can use Task Manager, Resource Monitor, Performance Monitor, and Event Viewer to track network-related events and statistics. This information will help you identify issues and determine the cause of an issue.

Network Tools and Utilities

INFORMATION IN THIS CHAPTER

- Local Security Policy
- Group Policy
- Security Configuration Wizard
- Command-Line Tools
- PowerShell Commands
- Other Relevant Tools

INTRODUCTION

Windows includes a number of tools and utilities for securing your environment. Some of these focused on the network, some provide overall system protection. For those tools and utilities that provide overall system protection, we will try to focus on the network security portion of those.

LOCAL SECURITY POLICY

The Local Security Policy is used to configure security and auditing policies that apply to the local machine. The policies range from account policies to IPSec policies to system audit policies. We won't be covering all of the policies, just those related to securing your network and auditing network access. We will look at the following sections: Local Policies, Network List Manager Policies, IP Security Policies on Local Computer, and Advanced Audit Policy Configuration.

Note: Windows Firewall with Advanced Security is covered in the Securing Network Access Chapter.

Local Policies

Local Policies are policies that apply to the local system. The Local Policies node contains three subnodes: Audit Policy, User Rights Assignment, and Security Options.

Audit Policy

The Audit Policy section is used to configure basic system auditing. The following audit policy options are ones you should consider configuring in order to be able to detect malicious network activity:

- *Audit object access:* This policy allows you to audit access to objects other than Active Directory objects.
- *Audit policy change:* This policy allows you to audit when changes are made to the audit policy.
- *Audit privilege use:* This policy allows you to audit when a user uses one of their user rights.
- *Audit process tracking:* This policy allows you to audit process actions like process creation and termination.
- *Audit system events:* This policy allows you to audit events like system startup and shutdown and system time change.

User Rights Assignment

The User Rights Assignment policies control who can perform which actions. It's important that you understand the ramifications of providing these rights. If an attacker were to gain these rights, they could take over the system or prevent others from accessing the system:

- *Access this computer from the network:* This policy controls who is allowed to access the system remotely through the network.
- *Add workstations to the domain*: This policy controls who can add computer accounts to the domain.
- *Allow log on through Remote Desktop Services:* This policy controls who can log into the system remotely using Remote Desktop Services.
- *Deny access to this computer from the network:* This policy specifically prevents users from being able to access the computer over the network. It will take precedence over the *Access this computer from the network* policy.
- *Deny log on through Remote Desktop Services:* This policy specifically prevents users from being able to access the system remotely through Remote Desktop Services. It will take precedence over the *Allow log on through Remote Desktop Services* policy.

- *Force shutdown from a remote system:* This policy controls who can remotely shut down the system.
- *Generate security audits:* This policy determines which accounts can add entries to the security logs.

Security Options

The Security Options section is a list of security settings that can be configured on the system. Most of these options can be configured via registry key, but having them all here makes them a lot easier to implement. There are many security options to choose from, but these ones that may be of particular interest:

Domain member: Digitally encrypt or sign secure channel data (always)—This option determines whether all secure channel traffic like NTLM coming from the domain controller must be signed or encrypted.

Domain member: Digitally encrypt secure channel data (when possible)—This option specifies whether a domain controller will attempt to negotiate encryption for secure channel traffic, such as NTLM.

Domain member: Digitally sign secure channel data (when possible)—This option specifies whether a domain controller will attempt to negotiate signing for secure channel traffic, such as NTLM.

Microsoft network client: Digitally sign communications (always)—This option specifies whether packet signing is required for SMB packets.

Microsoft network client: Digitally sign communications (if server agrees)—This option specifics whether digital signing will be attempted in SMB communications.

Microsoft network client: Send unencrypted password to third-party SMB servers—This option determines whether the SM redirector will send plaintext passwords to non-Microsoft SMB servers.

Microsoft network server: Amount of idle time required before suspending session—This option specifies how long an SMB session can be idle before it's suspended due to inactivity.

Microsoft network server: Attempt S4U2Self to obtain claim information—This option allows clients prior to Windows 8 to access files shares that use claims.

Microsoft network server: Digitally sign communications (always)—This option specifies whether SMB signing is required by the client.

Microsoft network server: Digitally sign communications (if client agrees)—The option specifies whether the server will attempt to negotiate SMB signing.

Microsoft network server: Disconnect clients when logon hours expire—This option specifies whether users connected to SMB shares will be disconnected when outside of valid logon hours.

Microsoft network server: Server SPN target name validation level—This option specifies the level of validation performed on an SPN that is provided by the client during an SMB session.

Network access: Allow anonymous SID/Name translation—This option determines whether anonymous users can request SID attributes for another user.

Network access: Do not allow anonymous enumeration of SAM accounts—This option determines whether Everyone will be replaced with Authenticated Users in resource permissions.

Network access: Do not allow anonymous enumeration of SAM accounts and shares—This option determines whether anonymous enumeration of SAM accounts and shares is allowed.

Network access: Do not allow storage of passwords and credentials for network authentication—This option determines whether Credential Manager will store passwords for domain authentication.

Network access: Let Everyone permissions apply to anonymous users—This option determines if the Everyone SID will be added to the token created for anonymous connections.

Network access: Named pipes that can be accessed anonymously—This option determines which pipes will allow anonymous access.

Network access: Remotely accessible registry paths—This option determines which registry keys can be accessed over the network.

Network access: Remotely accessible registry paths and sub-paths—This option determines which registry keys and subkeys can be accessed over the network.

Network access: Restrict anonymous access to Named Pipes and shares—This option restricts anonymous access to shares and pipes.

Network access: Shares that can be accessed anonymously—This setting determines which shares can be accessed by anonymous users.

Network access: Sharing and security model for local accounts—This option determines the authentication method for network logons that use local accounts.

Network security: Allow Local System to use computer identity for NTLM—This option allows Local System to revert to NTLM when using Negotiate.

Network security: Allow LocalSystem NULL session fallback—This option allows NTLM to fall back to NULL session when used with LocalSystem.

Network security: Allow PKU2U authentication requests to this computer to use online identities—This setting allows PKU2U authentication requests to this computer.

Network security: Configure encryption types allowed for Kerberos—This option allows you to specify the encryption types that will be used with Kerberos.

Network security: Do not store LAN Manager hash value on next password change—This option determines whether during the next password change the LAN Manager hash value for the new password will be stored.

Network security: Force logoff when logon hours expire—This option specifies if a user will be disconnected when the session falls outside of logon hours.

Network security: LAN Manager authentication level—This option determines which authentication protocol is used for network logons.

Network security: LDAP client signing requirements—This option sets the level of data signing required when clients make LDAP bind requests.

Network security: Minimum session security for NTLM SSP-based (including secure RPC) clients—This option requires this use of 128-bit encryption and/or NTLMv2 session security for clients.

Network security: Minimum session security for NTLM SSP-based (including secure RPC) servers—This option requires this use of 128-bit encryption and/or NTLMv2 session security for servers.

Network security: Restrict NTLM: Add remote server exceptions for NTLM authentication—This option creates an exception list of remote servers allowed to use NTLM authentication.

Network security: Restrict NTLM: Add server exceptions in this domain—This option allows you to specify a list of servers that are allowed to use NTLM authentication.

Network security: Restrict NTLM: Audit Incoming NTLM Traffic—This option allows you to log NTLM events for incoming traffic.

Network security: Restrict NTLM: Audit NTLM authentication in this domain—This option allows you to audit NTLM authentication from a domain controller.

Network security: Restrict NTLM: Incoming NTLM traffic—This option allows you to allow or deny NTLM authentication traffic.

Network security: Restrict NTLM: NTLM authentication in this domain—This option allows you to allow or deny NTLM authentication from a domain controller.

Network security: Restrict NTLM: Outgoing NTLM traffic to remote servers—This option allows you to deny or audit outgoing NTLM authentication traffic.

Network List Manager Policies

The Network List Manager node, as seen in Figure 7.1 allows you to configure options for the networks your system has connected to. You can also configure options for general network types like Unidentified Networks and All Networks (see Figure 7.1).

If you view the properties for a network, you bring up the network properties windows. The network properties window has three tabs: Network Name, Network Icon, and Network Location.

Network Name

The network name is used to identify the network. The Network Name tab, as seen in Figure 7.2, has two sections. In the Name section, you have two

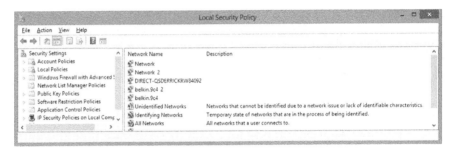

FIGURE 7.1 Network List Manager Policies

FIGURE 7.2 Network List Manager Network Name Tab

FIGURE 7.3 Network List Manager Network Icon Tab

options. You can manually specify a name for the network, or you can leave it as Not configured. In the User permissions section, you specify whether the user can change the network name or not.

Network Icon

The Network Icon tab, as seen in Figure 7.3, allows you to specify an icon to be used to denote the network. You can use an icon as a visual indicator of a potentially dangerous network. On the Network Icon tab, you can also specify whether the user can change the icon used for the network.

Network Location

The Network Location tab, as seen in Figure 7.4, is used to specify a location type for the network. Once a network has been assigned a network type, the appropriate firewall settings will automatically be applied. On the Network Local tab, you can also specify whether the user can change the network location.

IP Security Policies on the Local Computer

This section is used to configure IPSec policies and manage IP Filter lists.

To create an IP Security Policy, perform the following actions:

1. Right-click on the node and select Create IP Security Policy. This will bring up the IP Security Policy Wizard Welcome screen, as seen in Figure 7.5. Click Next.

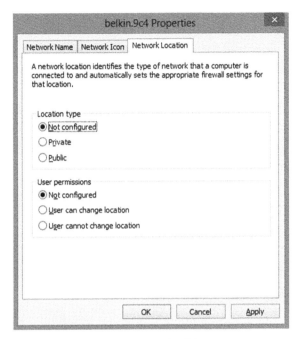

FIGURE 7.4 Network List Manager Network Location Tab

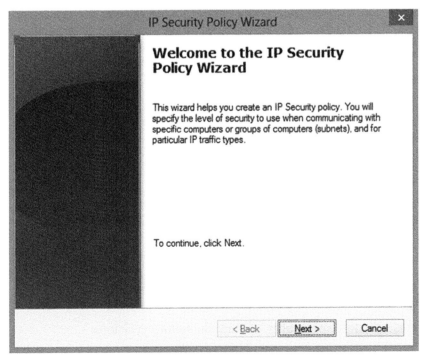

FIGURE 7.5 IP Security Policy Wizard Welcome Screen

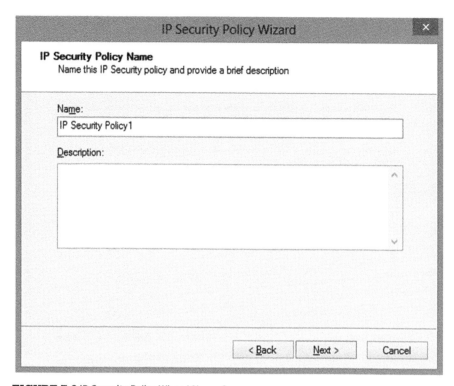

FIGURE 7.6 IP Security Policy Wizard Name Screen

2. This brings up the IP Security Policy Name screen, as seen in Figure 7.6. Enter a name for your new policy and click Next.
3. This brings up the Requests for Secure Communications screen, as seen in Figure 7.7. Here you can specify whether to use the IPSec default response rule. The default response rule dictates that security should be negotiated when no other rule exists. Click Next.
4. This brings up the Completing IP Security Policy screen, as seen in Figure 7.8. Click Finish.

IPSec policies are composed of IP filter lists and filter actions. IP filter lists define ports and protocols for interesting traffic. IP filter actions define what actions should be performed. To configure your IP filter lists and actions, right-click on IP Security Policies on Local Computer and select Manage IP filter lists and filter actions. This will bring up the Manager IP filter lists and filter actions window.

On the Manage IP Filter List tab, as seen in Figure 7.9, you can manage all the IP filter lists that you have created on the system and create new ones. The filters you see here can be used in any IPSec policy on the system.

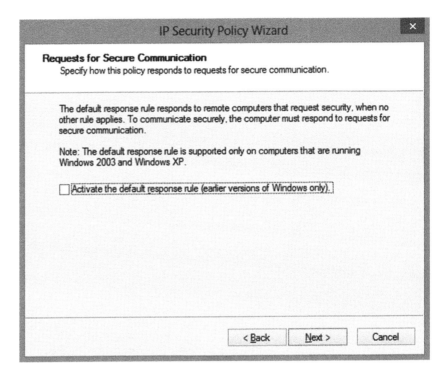

FIGURE 7.7 Request for Secure Communication Screen

On the Manage Filter Actions you can manage all the filter actions you have created and create new ones. These filter actions are available to all the IPSec policies on your system (see Figure 7.10).

Advanced Audit Policy Configuration

The Advanced Audit Policy Configuration section, as seen in Figure 7.11, allows for granular audit controls. The System Audit Policies—Local Group Policy Object node is where the configuration is done. Here is a listing of the audit policy options available:

- *Account Logon:* This section allows you to audit credential validation, account logon events, Kerberos authentication events, and Kerberos ticketing events.
- *Account Management:* This section allows you to audit changes to user accounts, groups, and computer accounts.
- *Detailed Tracking:* This section allows you to audit DPAPI, process creation, process termination, and RPC events.
- *DS Access:* This section allows you to audit Directory Service access, changes, and replication.

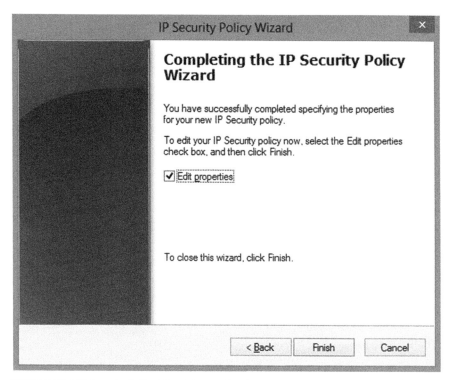

FIGURE 7.8 IP Security Policy Wizard Completion Screen

FIGURE 7.9 Manage IP Filter Lists Tab

FIGURE 7.10 Manage Filter Actions Tab

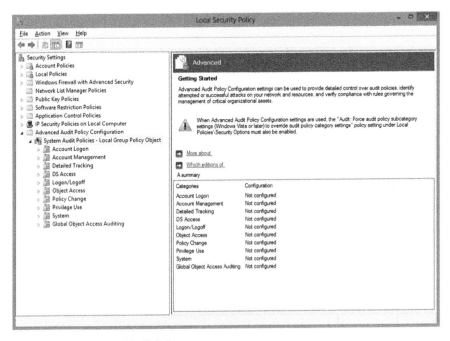

FIGURE 7.11 Advanced Audit Policy

- *Logon/Logoff:* This section allows you to audit account lockouts, IPSec events, logons, and logoffs.
- *Object Access:* This section allows you to audit file shares, certification services, the registry, kernel object access, and many other objects.
- *Policy Change:* This section allows you to audit changes in the authentication policy, authorization policy, and other policy change events.
- *Privilege Use:* This section allows you to audit the use of user privileges.
- *System:* This section allows you to audit the IPSec driver, security state changes, system integrity, and other system events.
- *Global Object Access Auditing:* This section allows you to audit registry and file system changes.

GROUP POLICY

Group Policy allows you to set configuration settings for multiple systems. Group Policy is implemented through Active Directory. Many of the options set in Group Policy are the same as those set through the Local Security Policy. We will go through and point out some of the policies you may want to consider setting.

Group Policy is broken into two nodes: Computer Configuration and User Configuration. Computer Configuration is for systems like desktops and servers. If a policy is configured for a computer, then everyone who log into that computer will receive the policy. User Configuration is for user accounts. If a policy is configured for a user, then the user will receive the policy no matter what system they log into.

Under Computer Configuration and User Configuration there are two subnodes: Policies and Preferences. Policies and Preferences are both used to set configuration settings. But, there is a difference between the two. When you set a policy, generally the user is not allowed to change the setting. But, when you set a preference, the user can go in and modify the setting. This allows you to make suggested modifications, but still allow the user some flexibility.

Computer Configuration > Policies > Windows Settings

Name Resolution Policy: This policy is used to configure DNS settings, DNSSEC, and Encoding.

Security Settings:

  Local Policies: This option was covered in the Local Security Policy section.
  System Services: This policy is used to configure which services should be enabled, disabled, or started automatically. You should make sure any service configured here is one that you have chosen to allow on your

network. You can also use this policy to force restricted services to be disabled.

Wired Network (802.3) *Policy:* This policy is used to configure network authentication, single sign-on, and usage of the Windows Wired Auto Config service.

Windows Firewall with Advanced Security: This option was covered in the Local Security Policy section.

Network List Manager Policies: This option was covered in the Local Security Policy section.

Wireless Network (*IEEE* 802.11) *Policies:* This option allows you to configure a set of wireless networks to which the client is allowed to connect. You can also configure general wireless settings like Prevent connections to ad hoc networks.

Network Access Protection: This option is used to create and manage enforcement clients. It's also used to enable NAP tracing.

IP Security Policies on Active Directory: Most of this option was covered under the Local Security Policy section. In addition, this policy has three default IPSec policies already configured: a respond only policy, a require security policy, and a request security policy.

Audit Policies: This option was covered in the Local Security Policy section.

Policy-based QoS: This node allows you to create and manage QoS policies. The policies are based on Differentiated Services Code Point (DSCP) values. Policies can be applied to all applications, specific executables, or requests to a particular URL.

Computer Configuration > Policies > Administrative Templates: Policy Definitions (ADMX Files) Retrieved from the Local Computer

Network: The Network node is used to configure settings for BITS, BranchCache, DNS Clients, TCPIP Settings, and other crucial network functionality.

System: The System node is used to configure settings for Internet Communication Management, Net Logon, Remote Assistance, and other crucial system functionality.

Windows Components: The Windows Components node includes setting for various Windows services like the ActiveX Installer Service, the Event Viewer Service, and Internet Explorer.

Computer Configuration > Preferences > Windows Settings

The Windows Settings node allows you to configure preferences for Applications, Drive Maps, Environment, Files, Folders, Ini Files, Registry, and Shortcuts.

Computer Configuration > Preferences > Control Panel Settings

The Control Panel Settings node allows to configure preferences for Data Sources, Devices, Folder Options, Internet Settings, Local Users and Groups, Network Options, Printers, Regional Options, Scheduled Tasks, and the Start Menu.

User Configuration > Policies > Windows Settings

Policy-based QoS: This node allows you to create and manage QoS policies. The policies are based on Differentiated Services Code Point (DSCP) values. Policies can be applied to all applications, specific executables, or requests to a particular URL.

User Configuration > Policies > Administrative Templates

Network: The Network node is used to configure settings for Network Connections, Offline Files, and Windows Connect Now.

System: The System node is used to configure settings for Folder Redirection, Internet Communication Management, and Logon .

Windows Components: The Windows Components node includes setting for various Windows services like the ActiveX Installer Service, the Event Viewer Service, and Internet Explorer.

Computer Configuration > Preferences > Windows Settings

The Windows Settings node allows you to configure preferences for Applications, Drive Maps, Environment, Files, Folders, Ini Files, Registry, and Shortcuts.

Computer Configuration > Preferences > Control Panel Settings

The Control Panel Settings node allows you to configure preferences for Data Sources, Devices, Folder Options, Internet Settings, Local Users and Groups, Network Options, Printers, Regional Options, Scheduled Tasks, and the Start Menu.

SECURITY CONFIGURATION WIZARD

The Security Configuration Wizard can help you improve the overall security of your systems and your network. It consists of a set of different smaller wizards that ask questions about services and applications that should be running on your system. You have the option to skip any of the smaller individual wizards you choose.

At the end of the Security Configuration Wizard, you will be presented with a recommended configuration. This recommended configuration includes services that should be running or disabled and various configuration settings.

Using the Security Configuration Wizard

Using the Security Configuration Wizard is a straightforward process. You simply proceed through the individual sections, answering the questions along the way. We will now go through the entire wizard:

1. The Welcome screen, as seen in Figure 7.12, will go over the purpose of the Security Configuration Wizard. Click Next.
2. On the Configuration Action screen as seen in Figure 7.13, you must specify what you want to do with the wizard. You can create a new security policy, edit an existing policy, apply an existing policy, or rollback the last applied security policy. For the purpose of this example, we will choose create a new security policy.
3. On the Select Server screen, as seen in Figure 7.14, you must choose the server you want to use as a baseline. Pick a server and click Next.

FIGURE 7.12 Security Configuration Wizard

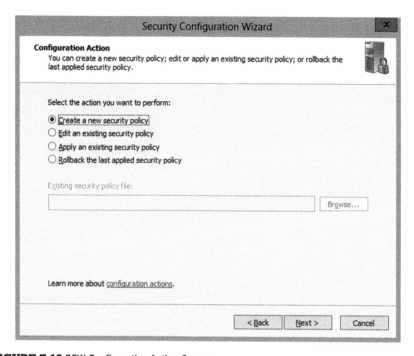

FIGURE 7.13 SCW Configuration Action Screen

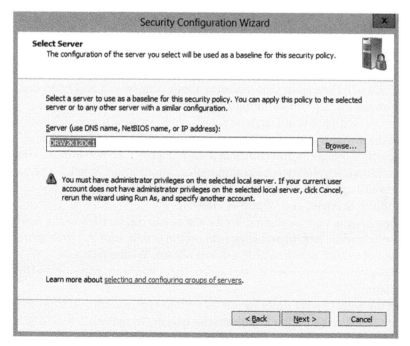

FIGURE 7.14 SCW Select Server Screen

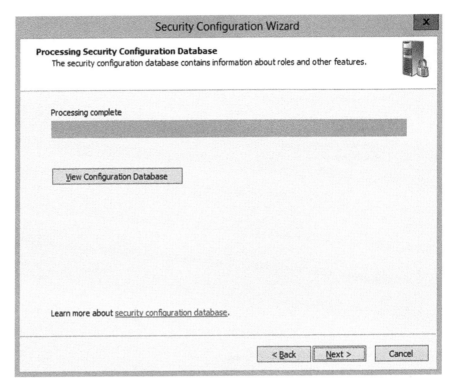

FIGURE 7.15 SCW Configuration Database Screen

4. While on the Configuration Database screen, as seen in Figure 7.15, the wizard will then gather information about your system and place the information in a configuration database.
5. On the Configuration Database screen, you can view the configuration database that was created. If you select View Configuration Database, the Security Configuration Wizard, as seen in Figure 7.16 will appear. Here you can view your system's configuration information. It will be presented in five categories: Server Roles, Client features, Administration and Other Options, Services, and Windows Firewall.
6. After viewing your configuration database, you can go back to the Security Configuration Wizard and click next on the Configuration Database screen.
7. The Role-Based Service Configuration wizard, as seen in Figure 7.17, allows you to specify what roles and services you want running on the system.
8. On the Select Server Roles screen, as seen in Figure 7.18, you need to select the roles you would like to run on the system. To make it a little easier, the wizard can show you which roles are currently installed on the system. Choose your roles and then click Next.

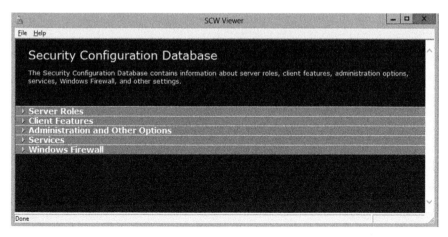

FIGURE 7.16 Security Configuration Database Viewer

FIGURE 7.17 SCW Role-Based Service Configuration

9. On the Select Client Features screen, as seen in Figure 7.19, you need to select the client features you would like to run on the system. To make it a little easier, the wizard can show you which client features are currently installed on the system. Choose your client features, and then click Next.

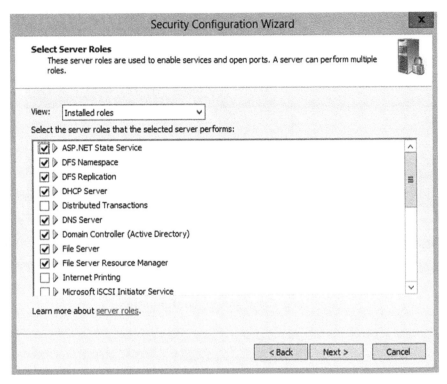

FIGURE 7.18 SCW Server Roles Screen

10. There are other application and service options that can be enabled on the system. The Administration and Other Options screen, as seen in Figure 7.20, allows you to select which options you want to run on the system. To make it easier, the wizard can show you which options you currently have running on the system. Choose your options and then click Next.

11. The Additional Services screen, as seen in Figure 7.21, allows you to specify what other services you want to have running on the system. Choose your services and then click Next.

12. Since you can create the baseline policy on one system, then apply the policy on another system, you may run into a situation where a target server is running a service that is not in the policy. The Unspecified Services screen, as seen in Figure 7.22, allows you to specify what would happen in cases such as those.

13. The Confirm Service Changes screen, as seen in Figure 7.23, details all the service changes that will be made as a result of the selections you made. Confirm the changes and then click Next.

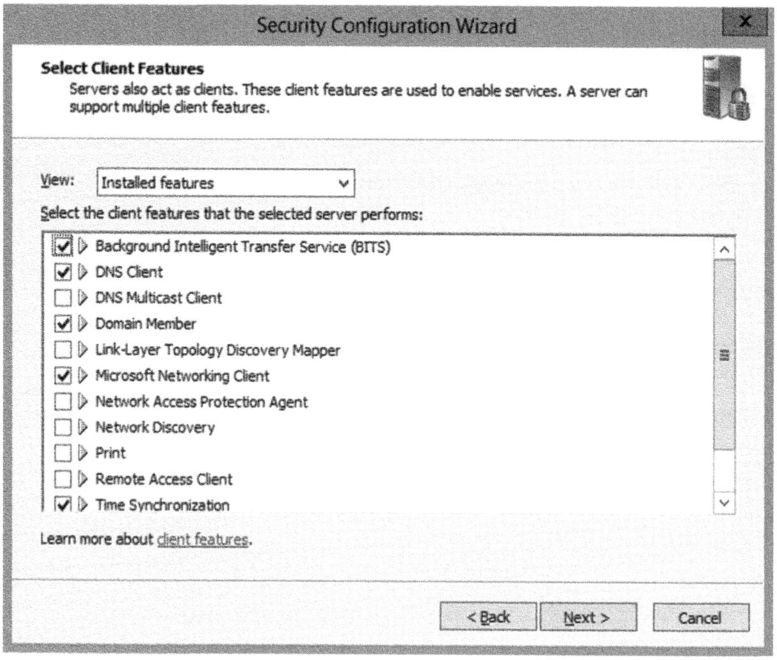

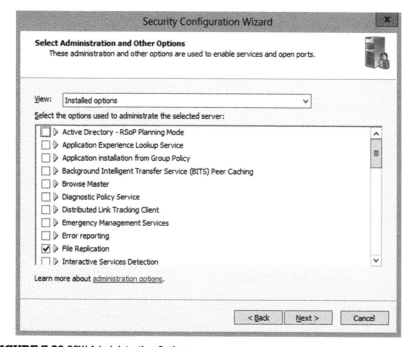

FIGURE 7.19 SCW Client Features Screen

FIGURE 7.20 SCW Administration Options

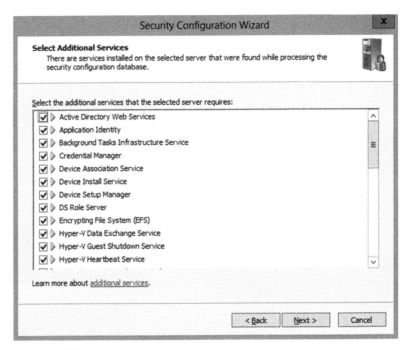

FIGURE 7.21 SCW Additional Services

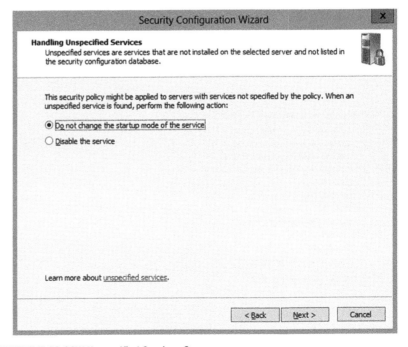

FIGURE 7.22 SCW Unspecified Services Screen

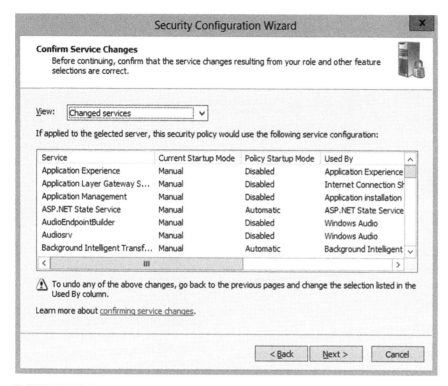

FIGURE 7.23 SCW Confirm Changes Screen

14. Next is the Network Security section of the Security Configuration Wizard, as seen in Figure 7.24. If you like, you can choose to skip this selection. Click Next.
15. The Network Security Rules screen, as seen in Figure 7.25, will list the Windows Firewall rules that need to be created in order to provide the services and features you enabled in the roles portion of the wizard. Confirm the rules you want enabled and then click Next.
16. Next is the Registry Settings section of the Security Configuration Wizard, as seen in Figure 7.26. If you choose, you can skip this section of the wizard. Click Next.
17. The SMB Security Signatures screen, as seen in Figure 7.27, allows you to configure whether SMB signatures are required. You are asked to select the clients that will be connecting and whether you want to sign file and print traffic.
18. On the LDAP Signing screen, as seen in Figure 7.28, you configure whether you want LDAP queries to be signed.

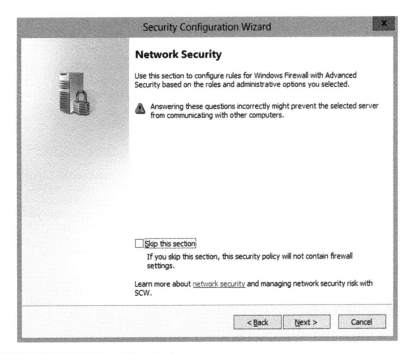

FIGURE 7.24 SCW Network Security Screen

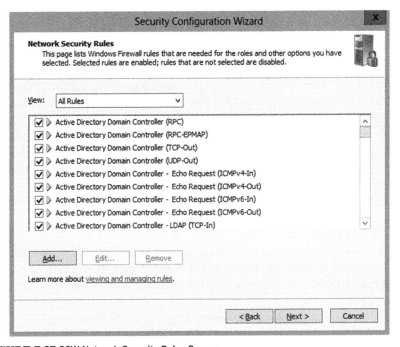

FIGURE 7.25 SCW Network Security Rules Screen

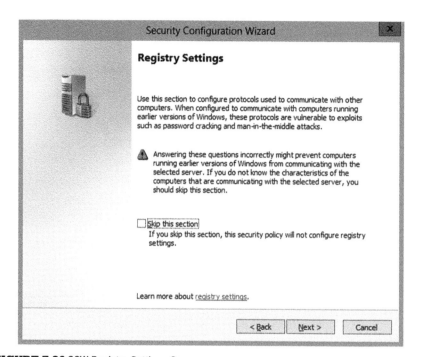

FIGURE 7.26 SCW Registry Settings Screen

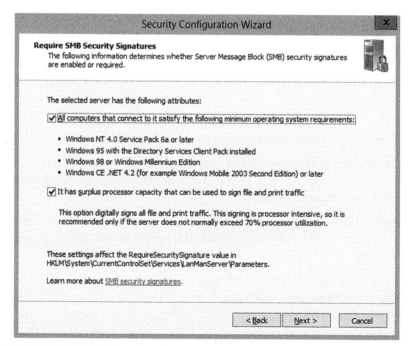

FIGURE 7.27 SCW SMB Signatures Screen

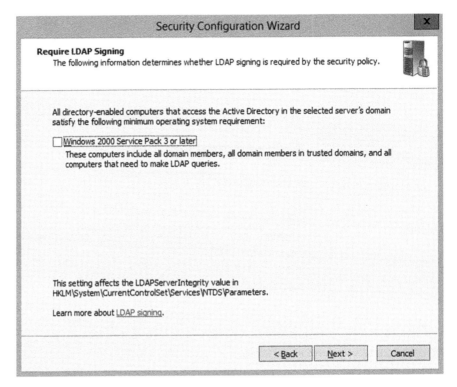

FIGURE 7.28 SCW LDAP Signing Screen

The Outbound Authentication Methods screen, as seen in Figure 7.29, allows you to configure which authentication methods the server can use when making outbound connections.

If you choose to use domain accounts for outbound authentication, then you will be prompted with another set of related questions, as seen in Figure 7.30.

On the Registry Settings Summary screen, as seen in Figure 7.31, you can review all the decisions you made in the Registry Settings section of the Security Configuration Wizard.

Next is the Audit Policy sections of the Security Configuration Wizard, as seen in Figure 7.32. In this section, you determine which events will be audited by your system.

On the System Audit Policy screen, as seen in Figure 7.33, you decide which events you want to enable auditing for. You can enable auditing for successful or unsuccessful activities.

On the Audit Policy Summary screen, as seen in Figure 7.34, you review the auditing settings that have been set.

FIGURE 7.29 SCW Outbound Authentication Screen

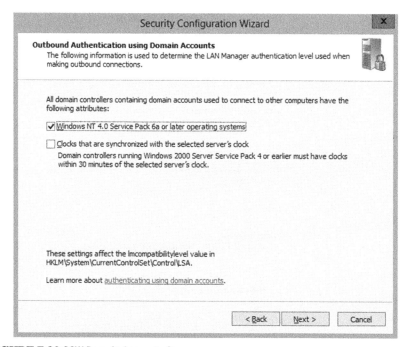

FIGURE 7.30 SCW Domain Accounts Screen

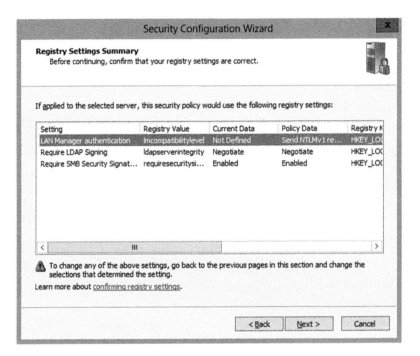

FIGURE 7.31 SCW Registry Settings Summary Screen

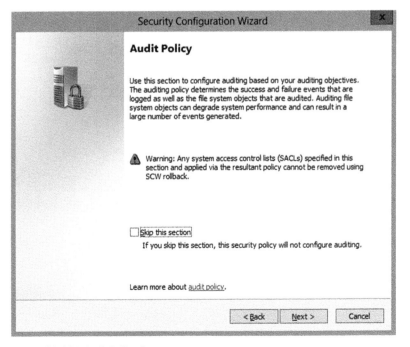

FIGURE 7.32 SCW Audit Policy Screen

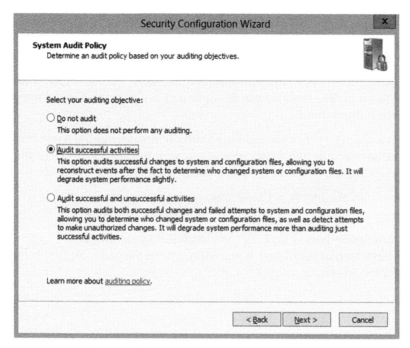

FIGURE 7.33 SCW System Audit Policy Screen

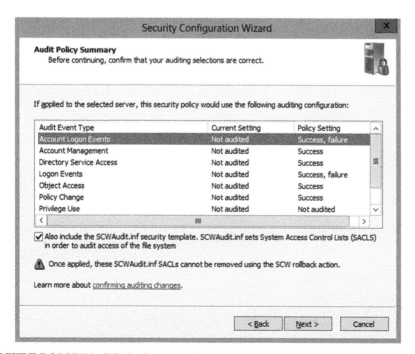

FIGURE 7.34 SCW Audit Policy Summary Screen

Next is the Save Security Policy section, as seen in Figure 7.35. In this section, you determine what should be done with the new security policy that has been created.

On the Security Policy File Name, as seen in Figure 7.36, you give your new policy a name. You can also use the Security Configuration Wizard viewer to view the policy settings.

Additionally, if you click the Include Security Templates button, it will bring up the Include Security Templates window, as seen in Figure 7.37. Here you can choose to include settings from any security templates you may have.

On the Apply Security Policy screen, as seen in Figure 7.38, you decide whether you want to apply the new policy right now or at a later time.

The Completing the Security Configuration Wizard screen, as seen in Figure 7.39, is the last screen of the wizard. If you chose to save the policy and apply later, it will tell you where the policy was saved.

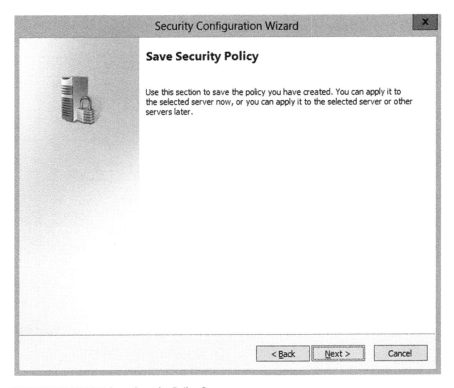

FIGURE 7.35 SCW Save Security Policy Screen

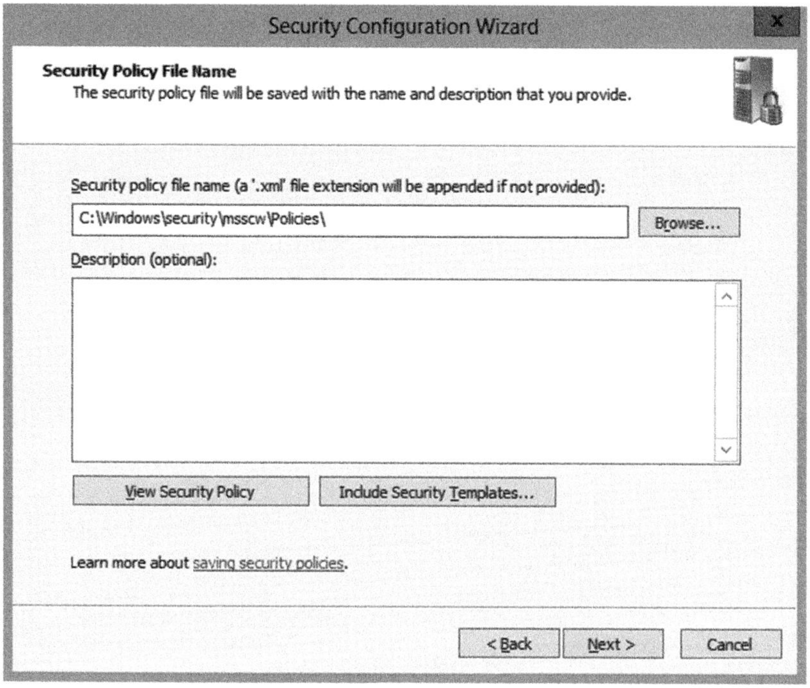

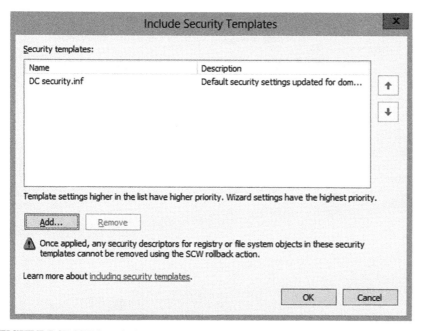

FIGURE 7.36 SCW Security Policy File Name Screen

FIGURE 7.37 SCW Security Templates Screen

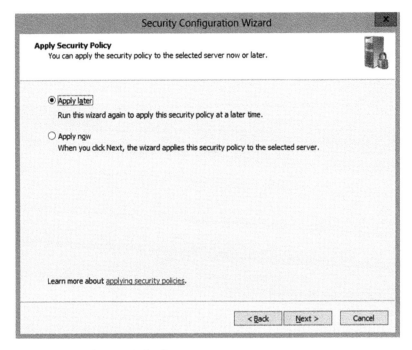

FIGURE 7.38 Apply Security Policy Screen

FIGURE 7.39 Security Configuration Wizard Screen

COMMAND-LINE TOOLS

There are a number of command-line tools that can be used for monitoring and protecting your systems. These simple tools can be used in scripts or with other more robust tools and frameworks to help provide a clearer picture of what's going on with your network.

Ipconfig

This tool is used to display and manipulate IP information on your system. You can display and control information for all adapters in the system or just specific adapters. The Ipconfig command without any options will show basic IP information. Here is a list of options available with the command:

/? This option will display the help for the command.
/all This option will display the full IP information.
/release This option will cause the IPv4 address for the adapter to be released.
/release6 This option will cause the IPv6 address for the adapter to be released.
/renew This option will renew IPv4 information for the specified adapter.
/renew6 This option will renew IPv6 information for the specified adapter.
/flushdns This option will clear the DNS cache on the system.
/registerdns This option will refresh your DHCP lease and re-register your DNS names.
/displaydns This option will display the contents of the system's DNS cache.
/showclassid This option displays all the DHCP class IDs allowed for the adapter.
/setclassid This option sets the DHCP class ID.
/showclassid6 This option displays all the IPv6 DHCP class IDs allowed for the adapter.
/setclassid6 This option sets the IPv6 DHCP class ID.

If you feel as though your system had been tampered with, Ipconfig can be useful. You can use this option to ensure that your system is configured the way you expect. You should check to ensure that your DNS server is configured how you would expect. Many different malware try to change the DNS configuration of a system so users can be directed to malicious site. Another way to check this is to view the DNS cache. If there is a cached entry that you do not expect, it might be a sign that something is wrong. If you do see an entry that shouldn't be there, you should try flushing the cache and checking to see if the entry is removed and whether it comes back or not.

Ping

Ping is the packet Internet groper utility. The ping command is used to test connectivity between two systems. It's also used to determine the round-trip time between two systems. Ping will also allow you to see if there is any packet loss in the connection between two systems. When you initiate the ping command, an ICMP echo request message will be sent to the target machine. The sender will then wait for an ICMP response from the target.

Many network- and system-based firewalls will block ICMP requests by default. This is because the ping command can be used to initiate a denial of service (DOS) attack. You can use ping to send a constant barrage of ICMP echo requests to a system; more than the target system can process and still remain stable. This type of attack is called a ping flood.

The following options are available with the ping command on Windows 8 and Windows Server 2012 systems:

-t This option specifies that the ping will continue until stopped. By default, with the ping command, only four echo requests are sent.
-a This option will cause the IP addressed to be resolved to a hostname.
-n This option specifies the number of echo requests to be sent.
-l This option specifies the size of the send buffer.
-f This option sets the don't fragment flag in the packet. If this flag is not set (IPv4 only).
-I This option sets the time to live.
-v This option sets the type of service.
-r This option records the number of hops (IPv4 only).
-s This option will record a timestamp for each hop (IPv-4 only).
-j This option specifies a loose source route (IPv4 only).
-k This option specifies a strict source route (IPv4 only).
-w This option specifies the timeout value. It controls how long the source system will wait for a response from the target system.
-R This option uses a routing header to test reverse route (IPv6 only).
-S This option specifies a source address to use for the ping command.
-4 This option forces the use of IPv4.
-6 This option forces the use of IPv6.

Tracert

The tracert command is Windows' version of traceroute. It is used for tracing the path between two systems. It will display the different routers or hops needed to travel from the source system to the destination system. Tracert will also show the time it takes to get from the source to the destination. The tracert command can help you determine if packets are taking an expected route to get to a remote system. For example, if you see packets leaving your network and going out to the Internet to get to a local system, that's a sign that something may be wrong. There tracert command can also help you determine where network slowness is occurring. There may be a router on your network that is processing traffic slower than usual.

The following options are available with the tracert command:

-d This option tells tracert not to resolve hostnames of the destination system and the hops. Tracert moves a little faster when it does not have to resolve the hostnames.
-h This option sets a maximum number of hops allowed before reaching the destinations. Once the maximum number of hops is reached, tracert will complete whether the destination has been reached or not.
-j This option enables loose source routing around a host list (IPv4 only).
-w This option is used to specify a timeout value for each reply.
-R This is an IPv6 option used to trace the round-trip path (IPv6 only).
-S This is an IPv6 option that allows you to specify the source address used for the request (IPv6 only).
-4 This option is used to force IPv6.
-6 This option is used to force IPv6.

Netstat

Netstat is used to show protocol information and current connection information. You can use netstat to view which systems your system currently has a connection with. If you see a connection that you do not expect, there may be an issue. Also, if you see more open sockets than you expect, your system may be the target of a TCP SYN attack:

-a This option displays all current connections and listening ports.
-b This option displays the executable associated with a listening port.
-e This option is used to show Ethernet statistics.
-f This option displays the FQDN for foreign addresses.
-n This option displays IP addresses and ports in numeric format.
-o This option displays the process ID associated with each connection.
-p This option only displays connections for the specified protocol.
-r This option displays the routing table for the system.
-s This option displays per protocol statistics.
-t This option displays the current connection offload state.
-x This option displays NetworkDirect connections, listeners, and shared endpoints.
-y This options displays the TCP connection template for all connections.

Interval: This option displays the current statistics, pausing for a given interval between displays.

NBTStat

The NBTStat is used to gather NetBIOS information and statistics. You can use NBTStat to investigate suspicious Windows-based systems. You can also use it to determine if your NBT cache may be corrupt or poisoned:

-a This option will display the remote machine's NetBIOS table given the machine's name.
-A This option will display the remote machine's NetBIOS table given the machine's IP address.
-c This option will display the NBT cache on the local system.
-n This option will list the local NetBIOS names.
-r This option will give statistics around names that have been resolved by the system.
-R This option is used to purge and reload the remote cache name table.
-S This option will display the sessions table with destination IP addresses.
-s This option will display the sessions table. It will convert the IP addresses to NetBIOS names.
-RR This option will send Name Release packets to the Windows. It will then initiate a NetBIOS refresh.

ARP

There are two definitions of ARP in play here. First of all, ARP is the Address Resolution Protocol. The ARP is used to translate IP addresses to MAC addresses. Second, there is the ARP command in Windows. This is what we're concerned about. The ARP command is used to get information about the ARP table on your system. This can help you to determine if your ARP table has been poisoned. The ARP command has the following options:

-a This option will display the current ARP table.
-g This option will display the current ARP table.
-v This option will display the current ARP table in verbose mode.
-N This option will display ARP entries for the network interface.
-d This option will delete the specified host from the cache. If you use an *, all addresses will be deleted.
-s This option is used to add an entry to the ARP table.

Getmac

The getmac command is used to query system MAC addresses. These addresses can be compared to the addresses that are listed in the ARP table. They should match. If not, there could be a problem. Without any options, getmac will show the physical addresses used by the network adapters in the system:

/S This option allows you to retrieve the physical addresses used by a remote system.

/U This option is used to specify the username that should be used when connecting to a remote system.

/P This option is used to specify the password that should be used when connecting to a remote system.

/FO This option is used to specify a format for the output. The options are table, list, and CSV. The default is to show the information in table format.

/NH This option specifies that the column header should not be shown in the output when using either table or CSV format.

/V This option specifies the use of verbose output.

/? This option is used to display the help for the command.

NET

The NET command comes with many different command options. It is used for a host of different network-related functions. Some are system based; some are user based. The options available with the NET command are as follows:

ACCOUNTS This option is used to change user and computer account settings.

COMPUTER This option is used to add computer to and remove them from the domain.

CONFIG This option is used to change workstation or server configuration settings.

CONTINUE This option is used to instruct a service to continue after it has been paused.

FILE This option will display shared files that are currently being used.

GROUP This option is used to manage group settings within a domain.

HELP This option is used to display help information. It can also be used with the individual command options.

HELPMSG This option can give you information about specific Windows messages.

LOCALGROUP This option is used to manage groups on the local system. If you specify a domain, you can also use it to manage domain-based groups.

PAUSE This option is used to instruct a service to pause.

SESSION This option is used to display network session connected to the local computer. This option can also be used to delete sessions.

SHARE This option is used to manage network shares.

START This option is used to instruct a service to start.

STATISTICS This option is used to display network statistics.

STOP This option is used to instruct a service to stop.

TIME This option is used to display the time and date on a remote computer.

USE This option is used to connect to or disconnect from a network share.

USER This option is used to display and manage user accounts on the system.

VIEW This options displays the shared resources on the system.

Pathping

The pathping command is similar to the tracert command. It's used to show the path from the source computer to the destination computer. When the command is typed by itself, then help information will be displayed. Here is a list of options available with the command:

-g This option enables loose source routing.

-h This option specifies a maximum number of hops when trying to reach the target.

-i This option allows to specify a source address to be used with the command.

-n This option specifies that hostnames should not be resolved.

-p This option is used to specify a wait time between pings.

-q This option is used to specify the number of queries per hop.

-w This option is used to specify a wait timeout for each reply.

-4 This option is used to force IPv4.

-6 This option is used to force IPv6.

Route

The route command is used to control the network routing table on your system. You can view the current routing table, add routes, or delete routes. Many times you will find that your system is having trouble reaching a destination because of an invalid routing table entry. If you used tracert to find out the route your system is using to get to a destination system is wrong, you might want to use the route command to view your systems routing table to ensure that there are no invalid entries. Some viruses or malware will create routing table entries on your system that will direct your system's network traffic to a particular interface or site.

The route command includes the following options:

-f This option will clear all gateway entries out of the routing table.

-p This option is used with the ADD command. It will cause a route to be persistent. Without it, a routing table entry that is manually added will not be persistent after a system reset.

-4 This option forces the use of IPv4.

-6 This option forces the use of IPv6.

Command There are four commands that can be used: PRINT, ADD, DELETE, and CHANGE. PRINT will display the current routing table. ADD will allow you to add an entry to the routing table. CHANGE will allow you to modify an entry in the routing table.

Destination This option specifies the destination host.

MASK This option is used to specify that the next value entered will be the subnet mask.

Netmask This variable represents the subnet mask.

Gateway This variable represents the gateway address.

Interface This variable represents the network interface that will be used for the route.

METRIC This option specifies the metric for the route.

NETSH

NETSH is a powerful command-line network management utility. The NETSH utility is architected in a hierarchy. At the top-level context is the base NETSH command functionality. At the next level is functionality for different network management interfaces. These interfaces are called sub-contexts. For example, there is a context for DHCP client. You can use that context to manage different aspects of your DHCP client.

NETSH Context Commands

Add: This option will add configuration entries. It can also be used to add helper DLLs.

Delete: This option will remove configuration entries. It can also be used to remove helper DLLs.

Dump: This option will dump configuration information to a script. This script will be used later to restore the configuration.

Exec: This option runs a script file.

Help: This option displays a list of commands.

Set: This option updates configuration settings. You can use it to set the machine on which to operate.

Show: This option displays information about aliases and top-level helpers.

NETSH Sub-Contexts

There are two ways to access sub-contexts commands. You can type netsh <context> command. Or, at the command prompt type NETSH to enter interactive mode. Then enter the name of the context you would like to access:

advfirewall: This sub-context is for Windows Firewall with Advanced Security. You can use it to add and delete firewall rules and make other changes to your Windows Firewall configuration.

branchcache: This sub-context is for configuring the BranchCache feature. You can use it to manage your cache and your content information keys.

bridge: This sub-context is for network bridging.

dhcpclient: This sub-context for your system's DHCP client component. You can use it to enable or disable tracing. You can also use it to dump trace files.

Dnsclient: This sub-context is for your system's DNS client component. You can use it to modify and dump configuration files.

firewall: This sub-context is for Windows Firewall. You can use it to modify and dump configuration files. It is recommended that you use the advfirewall sub-context instead of this one.

http: This sub-context is for Windows Firewall. You can use it to modify and dump configuration files. You can also use it to flush internal buffers for log files.

Interface: This sub-context is used for network interface management. You can use it to configure interface, proxies, and tunnels.

ipsec: This sub-context is used for IPSec configuration. You can use it to manage policies, filters, and actions.

lan: This sub-context is for Local Area Networks. You can use it to configure interface settings and export LAN profiles.

Mbn: This sub-context is for mobile broadband networks. You can use it to connect to and disconnect from a mobile broadband network.

Namespace: This sub-context is for the DNS namespace. You can use it to display configuration information.

nap: This sub-context is for Network Access Protection. You can use it to manage your NAP client configuration.

netio: This sub-context is for network input output. You can use it to modify and dump configuration information.

p2p: This sub-context is for peer-to-peer networking. You can use it to manage collaboration and identity management.

ras: This sub-context is for Remote Access services. You can use it to manage remote access configuration and diagnostics.

rpc: This sub-context is for Remote Procedure Call. You can use it to manage bindings and subnet information.

trace: This sub-context is for trace files. You can use it to start and stop tracing, and do conversions on trace files.

wcn: This sub-context is for Windows Connect Now. You can use it to connect to a wireless network and query information from a wcn device.

wfp: This sub-context is for Windows Filtering Platform. You can use it to view real-time diagnostics information and settings diagnostics options.

winhttp: This sub-context is for Windows HTTP. You can use it to configure WinHTTP settings and proxy information.

winsock: This sub-context is for Windows Sockets. You can use it to manage WinSOCK and LSP configuration.

Wlan: This sub-context is for wireless LAN. You can use it to connect to ` wireless networks and configure diagnostics and tracing.

POWERSHELL COMMANDS

An increasing amount of Windows system management is done using Windows PowerShell. PowerShell is a powerful script language that can be used to automate installation, configuration, and management of Windows systems. Windows PowerShell commands are organized into modules. Modules contain a number of different commandlets. In this section will go over some PowerShell commands that may help you in your network management and troubleshooting.

General Networking

There are many PowerShell modules available for general network configuration. Two of the more prominent are NetAdapter and NetTCPIP. NetAdapter lets you view and configure information related to the network adapters installed in your system. NetTCPIP lets you configure the TCP/IP protocol.

Here are some useful PowerShell general networking commands.

List IP Addresses:
```
Get-WmiObject -Class Win32_NetworkAdapterConfiguration -Filter
IPEnabled=TRUE -ComputerName. | Select-Object -Property IPAddress
```

Show network adapter information:
```
Get-WmiObject -Class Win32_NetworkAdapterConfiguration -Filter
IPEnabled=TRUE –ComputerName
```

Configure a static IP address:
```
New-NetIPAddress -IPAddress 10.0.0.2 -InterfaceAlias "Ethernet"
-DefaultGateway 10.0.0.1 -AddressFamily IPv4 -PrefixLength 24
```

Set DNS address:
> Set-DnsClientServerAddress -InterfaceAlias "Ethernet" -ServerAddresses 10.10.10.1

Join a computer to a domain:
> Add-Computer -DomainName zomg.local

Network Management

PowerShell is also a useful management tool. In large environments, automation can help ease the administrative burden. Powershell offers a complete set of tools for installation, configuration, and management.

Here are some useful PowerShell network management commands.

Create a DNS Foreward lookup zone:
> Add-DnsServerPrimaryZone -Name "derrick.com" -ZoneFile "derrick.com. dns"

Create a DNS Reverse lookup zone:
> Add-DnsServerPrimaryZone 0.0.10.in-addr.arpa -ZoneFile 0.0.10.in-addr. arpa.dns

Perform an install using an exported configuration:
> Install-WindowsFeature-ConfigurationPathFile <exportedconfig.xml>

Install DHCP Server role:
> Install-WindowsFeature DHCP -IncludeManagementTools

To authorize a DHCP server:
> Add-DhcpServerInDC -DnsName server.dns.local

Add DHCP Server scope:
> Add-DhcpServerv4Scope -name "Scope1" -StartRange 10.0.0.1 -EndRange 10.0.0.254 -SubnetMask 255.255.255.0 –State Active

OTHER RELEVANT TOOLS

There are a number of useful downloadable utilities that were compatible with previous versions of Windows. I don't know if newer versions will be released that are officially compatible with Windows 8 and Windows Server 2012. But, I will give a brief overview of some of them, so you know what they are and can be on the lookout for them.

PortQry

PortQry is a port scanner. The original tool, portqry, is command-line based tool. There is also a newer UI-based version called PortQRYUI. They are both available for download from the Microsoft website. You can use the tool to help troubleshoot TCP/IP connectivity issues. PortQry will report status for ports on a remote computer as listening, not listening, or filtered.

Microsoft Security Compliance Manager

The Security Compliance Manager is a free tool available for download from the Microsoft website. It includes policies and DCM (Desired Configuration Management) configuration packs. These are based on industry best practices and Microsoft Security Guide recommendations. You can view, update, and export security baselines. You can deploy your packages to domain systems and non-domain systems.

Microsoft Baseline Security Analyzer

The Microsoft Baseline Security Analyzer will examine your system and identity security issues. It will do a vulnerability assessment to check for system misconfigurations. It will also examine your system to check for missing security updates and service packs. You can use the Microsoft Baseline Security Analyzer to examine both local and remote systems. The tool offers both a command-line interface and a GUI.

Enhanced Mitigation Experience Toolkit

The Enhanced Mitigation Experience Toolkit helps prevent security vulnerabilities from being exploited. It does this by using threat mitigation technologies. With the Enhanced Mitigation Experience Toolkit, you specify a specific executable to be protected. The EMET will prevent the executable from performing what it considers suspicious actions.

Attack Surface Analyzer

The Attack Surface Analyzer will scan your system to determine the attack surface. The Attack Surface Analyzer will take a snapshot of your system before and after software installation; then identify changes in the attack surface. This will help you understand the effects of the applications you install. This allows you to determine what security changes need to be made after an application is installed.

SUMMARY

There are several tools available for securing your Windows systems. The Local Security Policy application is used to configure security settings on a local system. Group Policy is used to configure security policies on all the systems in your Active Directory domain. The Microsoft Security Configuration Wizard asks you a series of questions to help you configure a comprehensive security policy for your systems. In addition to these tools there are a multitude of command-line tools and Windows PowerShell tools to configure and manage different aspects of your system configuration.

Index

Printed and bound by CPI Group (UK) Ltd, Croydon, CR0 4YY

03/10/2024

01040343-0005